CRIMINAL PRACTICE

BY ANASTASIA & ANDREW VIALICHKA

First Edition

Published by MetExam
https://metexam.co.uk

(m)etexam

ISBN: 978-1-917053-15-0

ISBN: 978-1-917053-23-5 (Hardcover)

This publication is designed exclusively for educational purposes, serving as a comprehensive study aid for individuals preparing for the SQE 1 examination. It should not be construed as offering legal advice or as an authoritative resource on legal matters. Its primary objective is to facilitate learning and exam preparation.
Authors: Vialichka, Anastasia; Vialichka, Andrew
Title: Criminal Practice. SQE 1 Prep Course/Anastasia Vialichka, Andrew Vialichka
Description: First Edition. | London: MetExam, 2024.
Identifiers: ISBN 978-1-917053-15-0
Subjects: LCSH Criminal Practice—England—Examinations, questions, etc. | Criminal Practice—Wales—Examinations, questions, etc. | Common law—England—Examinations, questions, etc.| Legal education—England. | Legal education—Wales.

INTRODUCTION

Welcome to the Criminal Practice Law Guide, a comprehensive resource designed to aid your preparation for the SQE1 (Solicitors Qualifying Examination) exam. This guide is meticulously crafted to align with the SQE1 syllabus, providing a thorough overview of the legal frameworks, principles, and regulations governing legal services in the UK.

Each section of this guide is structured to enhance your learning experience, offering clear explanations, relevant legal precedents, and practical examples that mirror real-life scenarios you may encounter in your legal career. Additionally, we have included exam-focused insights and tips to help you effectively tackle the SQE1 assessment.

Best of luck in your studies and your future endeavours in the legal profession. Let's begin this journey together.

Throughout this text, authors draw upon a wealth of legal scholarship and case law. While specific contributions are not cited in the body of the book, a comprehensive list of all works referenced can be found at the end. These references serves as an acknowledgment of the significant works that have informed this text and as a resource for readers seeking to explore the subject matter further.

CHAPTER 1. THE FRAMEWORK OF CRIMINAL JUSTICE

1. Identifying a Suspect

In the jurisdiction of England and Wales, the responsibility for probing into criminal deeds is vested in the police force, tasked with forwarding cases for prosecution by the Crown Prosecution Service, which acts on behalf of the governmental authority.

The investigative process commences upon the suspicion of unlawful conduct, leading to the police undertaking inquiries. If evidence substantiates an individual's involvement in the crime, this individual is detained.

After this detention, a more thorough investigation unfolds, potentially involving interrogating the arrested individual. Should the Crown Prosecution Service judge there be a credible chance of a conviction being achieved, it will then move to accuse the individual of the crime formally.

2. The Accused

Upon formal accusation, the individual previously known as the 'suspect' transitions to the status of 'defendant' and is thus integrated into the judicial system.

This system is characterised by its adversarial nature, setting the stage for a confrontation between the defendant—who may be represented by legal counsel, such as a solicitor or barrister—and the prosecution. The onus is on the prosecution to persuade the court, beyond a shadow of a doubt, of the defendant's guilt regarding the alleged crime.

Conversely, the defence's objective is to introduce a level of doubt concerning at least one aspect of the crime attributed to the defendant. Success on the defence's part means the court cannot confidently assert the defendant's guilt, necessitating an 'acquittal'. It's crucial to understand that an acquittal does not imply the court's conviction of the defendant's innocence; rather, it signifies the court's inability to ascertain guilt beyond a reasonable doubt.

3. Offence Classification

Within the legal system, offences are sorted into one of three distinct groups: summary offences, triable either way or indictable offences.

Summary Offences are identified as the least severe category of crimes, with examples including minor instances of assault or battery. These are adjudicated solely in the Magistrates' Court, barring situations where they accompany more severe allegations and typically result in lesser penalties.

Indictable Offences constitute the most severe category, covering acts such as robbery and murder. Such offences are prosecuted exclusively in the Crown Court, meriting the most severe penalties available under the law. This designation is derived from the procedural use of an indictment to charge the accused in the Crown Court formally.

Offences Triable Either Way offer a degree of prosecutorial discretion, allowing for proceedings in either the Magistrates' Court or the Crown Court, depending on factors like the offence's gravity and the accused's preferences. Offences falling into this category, including theft and criminal damage, sit on the spectrum between summary and indictable offences in terms of their seriousness.

4. Primary Courts for Criminal Trials

4.1 The Magistrates' Court

In England and Wales, the initial courts for criminal trials are the Magistrates' Court and the Crown Court, with the former typically handling cases first. The Magistrates' Court operates under the guidance of either a District Judge or a bench of magistrates. A District Judge, a legally qualified professional who typically boasts a minimum of seven years of legal practice, either as a solicitor or barrister, conducts proceedings alone.

Conversely, magistrates, who are non-professional lay individuals, deliberate in groups of two or three, assisted by a legal advisor on legal and procedural queries. Within the Magistrates' Court, whether presided over by a District Judge or a panel of magistrates, the responsibility for determining matters of fact and law rests solely with them.

This includes decisions on the admissibility of evidence, which, once deemed inadmissible, must be disregarded in their further considerations of the case.

A local shopkeeper reports a shoplifting case in a small town in England. The suspect, Alex, is accused of stealing goods valued under £200. Given the nature of the offence, this case is classified as a summary offence and is thus scheduled for a hearing in the local Magistrates' Court.

On the day of the trial, the courtroom is presided over by a panel of three magistrates, as the offence does not require the expertise of a District Judge. The magistrates come from various non-legal professional backgrounds but have undergone training to adjudicate in the Magistrates' Court. A qualified legal professional advisor sits nearby to assist the magistrates with any legal questions during the proceedings, ensuring that the trial adheres to the correct legal standards and procedures.

As the trial commences, the prosecution presents evidence against Alex, including CCTV footage and witness testimonies from the shop staff. Alex's defence solicitor argues that the evidence needs to be more conclusive and challenge the reliability of the CCTV footage.

The magistrates listen attentively to both sides. During their deliberation, they consult the legal advisor on the point of law regarding the admissibility of a witness's testimony that seemed biased. The legal advisor explains the relevant legal principles, helping the magistrates to make an informed decision. After considering the legal advisor's input, the magistrates decide that the testimony in question does not meet the criteria for admissibility and, therefore, disregards it in their final decision-making process.

Ultimately, the magistrates conclude that, without the disputed testimony, the remaining evidence is not strong enough to convict Alex beyond a reasonable doubt. They decide to acquit Alex, explaining that while they are not convinced beyond a reasonable doubt of Alex's guilt, this does not necessarily mean they believe Alex is innocent of the charge. It simply means that the prosecution still needs to meet the high standard of proof required for a conviction.

This example demonstrates the Magistrates' Court process, highlighting the magistrates' roles, the District Judge (by comparison), and the legal advisor in ensuring that trials are conducted fairly and according to the law.

4.2 Superior Criminal Court

The Superior Criminal Court, more commonly known as the Crown Court, is overseen by a judge responsible for all legal rulings within the court. Decisions on factual matters, such as the guilt or innocence of the defendant, are exclusively the jury's purview.

This jury consists of twelve individuals chosen through a random selection process. Notably, the acquittal rate in the Crown Court is higher than that in the Magistrates' Courts, a phenomenon often attributed to the jury's involvement.

Cases within the Crown Court's remit include:

(a) **Serious Crimes:** These are strictly indictable offences, necessitating the formal environment and comprehensive legal processes of the Crown Court.

(b) **Flexible Jurisdiction Offences:** When a case involves offences that could be tried in either the Magistrates' Court or the Crown Court, but either the lower court decides it is beyond its capabilities or the defendant expresses a preference for a jury trial, the case moves to the Crown Court.

(c) **Associated Offences:** If either way or summary offence is directly related to a severe crime already under consideration by the Crown Court, especially if it involves potential imprisonment or disqualification from driving, it will be tried within the same court.

(d) **Appeal Hearings:** The Crown Court also serves as the venue for appeals against convictions or sentences imposed by the Magistrates' Court, offering a secondary review and the opportunity to reverse earlier decisions.

Jordan is charged with a serious crime of armed robbery, an offence categorised under severe crimes that are indictable only. Due to the severity of the charge, the case bypasses the Magistrates' Court and is directly referred to the Superior Criminal Court for trial. At the Crown Court, a judge is appointed to oversee the legal aspects of the trial, ensuring that the proceedings adhere to the law and that the defendant's rights are protected.

As the trial begins, a jury of twelve members is empanelled to determine the facts of the case. These jurors are randomly selected citizens who will assess the evidence presented by both the prosecution and the defence. The prosecution must present compelling evidence to convince the jury beyond a reasonable doubt of Jordan's guilt.

Evidence, including surveillance footage, witness testimonies, and forensic reports, are presented during the trial. Jordan's defence solicitor argues that the evidence is circumstantial and raises questions about its reliability and the identification process.

After hearing all the evidence and the closing arguments from both sides, the jury retreats to deliberate on the verdict. After several hours of discussion, they returned to the courtroom and announced a not-guilty verdict, leading to Jordan's acquittal. The jury's decision underscores the principle that if there's any reasonable doubt regarding the defendant's guilt, the verdict must be in favour of the defendant.

In a separate but related appeal case, Jamie, convicted in the Magistrates' Court for a minor related offence of receiving stolen goods from the same robbery, appeals the conviction on insufficient evidence. The appeal is heard in the Superior Criminal Court, where the judge reviews the legal basis of the original trial and decides to overturn Jamie's conviction, citing a misinterpretation of the evidence by the Magistrates' Court.

This fictional scenario showcases the Crown Court's critical role in adjudicating serious offences and its capacity to handle appeals from the Magistrates' Court, emphasising the importance of the jury in the justice process and the court's function in ensuring fair review and rectification of lower court decisions.

CHAPTER 2. LEGAL COUNSEL AT THE PO-LICE STATION

1. Entitlements of Detained Individuals During Interrogation

When an individual is held for questioning at a police station, they are afforded several protections and entitlements under the Police and Criminal Evidence Act 1984 (PACE). These fundamental rights are designed to ensure the detainee's welfare and fairness during detention.

The **primary rights** include:

(a) **Access to Legal Representation:** Detainees are entitled to consult with a solicitor free of charge, alongside the provision of medical assistance and interpretation services at no cost, ensuring that all suspects, regardless of financial status or language proficiency, can understand the proceedings and make informed decisions.

(b) **Notification of Detainment:** The right to inform a family member, friend, or another relevant individual of their arrest, ensuring that others know their situation and can take appropriate action if necessary.

(c) **Review of Police Conduct Guidelines:** Detainees have the right to examine the Codes of Practice, which detail the powers and responsibilities of the police under PACE, allowing individuals to understand the legal framework governing their detention.

(d) **Right to Remain Silent:** This right allows the detainee to avoid answering questions that may incriminate them, a crucial aspect of the legal protection against self-incrimination.

(e) **Awareness of Arrest Reasons:** Ensuring that individuals are informed about the reasons for their arrest and detention, providing transparency and allowing for the possibility of contesting any unlawful or unjustified detainment.

(f) **Inspection of Arrest and Detention Records:** The right to view documents related to their arrest and ongoing detention offers additional transparency and accountability.

(g) **Detention Time Limit Information:** Detainees must be informed about the maximum duration they can be held before being charged or released, preventing indefinite detention without charge.

These rights are integral to maintaining the integrity of the legal process and protecting individuals from potential abuses of power during the critical early stages of criminal investigations.

1.1 Entitlement to Legal Consultation

Any individual detained by the police is guaranteed the right to seek confidential legal counsel at any stage of their detention. This counsel, which remains impartial from police and prosecutorial influence, may be conducted via telephone or face-to-face consultation.

Upon the detainee's request for legal advice, the Defence Solicitors Call Centre (DSCC) is notified, except when the detainee opts for privately funded advice. The DSCC assesses the situation to decide if advice over the phone suffices or if the presence of a solicitor at the station is warranted.

However, access to this right can be temporarily withheld under **specific circumstances**, including:

(a) **The individual is detained** for an indictable or triable offence either way.

(b) **A high-ranking police officer,** at least of superintendent rank, approves the postponement in writing.

(c) **There are substantial grounds to believe** that allowing immediate legal consultation could lead to the tampering with evidence, obstruction of justice, alerting of other suspects, or impede the recovery of property connected to the offence.

This postponement is capped at a maximum of 36 hours. It's worth noting that delays in providing legal advice are exceptionally uncommon, given the critical nature of this right. Any failure to facilitate prompt access to legal counsel could significantly impact the legitimacy of any evidence gathered before providing such advice.

1.2 Notification of Detainment

Detainees can inform a chosen individual—a family member, friend, or acquaintance—about their arrest.

However, this entitlement may be temporarily withheld under **certain conditions:**

(a) The detainment is due to an offence categorised as either indictable only or triable either way.

(b) An officer holding the rank of inspector or higher approves the postponement through a written directive.

(c) There exists a justified belief that allowing this communication could disrupt the investigation, for example, by tampering with evidence, obstructing the investigation, notifying other individuals implicated in the offence, or impeding the retrieval of property associated with the crime.

This communication delay is limited to a maximum duration of 36 hours, intended to last only as long as necessary to safeguard the integrity of the ongoing investigation. Any decision to delay must be carefully measured to ensure it remains proportionate to the investigative needs.

Right to Legal Advice:

Sophie is arrested on suspicion of involvement in a severe burglary, an offence triable either way. Upon arrival at the police station, she asserts her right to legal advice.

The custody officer contacts the Defence Solicitors Call Centre (DSCC) to arrange for a solicitor to provide guidance. Sophie requests a specific solicitor she knows, and the officer facilitates this, ensuring Sophie can speak to her solicitor on the phone immediately and arranging for the solicitor to visit her at the station as soon as possible.

In a twist, the investigating officer suspects Sophie's solicitor might inadvertently pass information to co-suspects still at large. The officer, holding the rank of superintendent, authorises a written delay of Sophie's right to face-to-face legal advice, citing the risk of alerting other suspects as the reason. This delay lasts as long as necessary to secure critical evidence. It is capped at 36 hours, although the postponement lasts only 12 hours in practice until the risk is mitigated.

Right to Have Someone Informed of Arrest:

Michael is detained under suspicion of an indictable-only offence, specifically, armed robbery. He wishes to inform his partner of his arrest, asserting his right to communication. However, given the nature of Michael's alleged crime and the ongoing investigation, the police have concerns that notifying his partner could lead to other suspects being tipped off or crucial evidence being destroyed.

An inspector reviews the case details and, believing there's a substantial risk to the investigation's integrity, authorises a written delay of Michael's right to inform his partner. This decision is based on reasonable grounds, including the potential for interference with evidence and alerting other suspects involved in the robbery.

The delay is enforced for 24 hours, during which the police conduct urgent inquiries and secure vital evidence. After this period, and once the immediate risk to the investigation has subsided, Michael is allowed to exercise his right, and his partner is informed of his detention.

These scenarios demonstrate the practical application of detainees' rights and the exceptional circumstances under which these rights may be temporarily withheld to ensure the integrity of criminal investigations, always within the legal framework provided by PACE.

2. Detention Duration Parameters

The foundational guideline stipulates that a detainee cannot be held for more than 24 hours without charge, commencing from the moment they are brought into the police station.

Any detention extending beyond this period without formal charges is deemed illegal, necessitating either the charging or release of the individual within this timeframe.

2.1 Procedure for Extending Detention

An extension of up to an additional 12 hours, extending the total detention limit to 36 hours, is permissible under **specific circumstances:**

(a)   **The detention pertains to an individual suspected of committing a crime** that is either indictable only or triable either way.

(b) **A high-ranking officer**, at minimum a superintendent, **approves the extension of the detention period.**

(c) There is a substantiated belief that **additional time in custody is essential for gathering more evidence** or further interrogation that could significantly impact the case.

(d) **The inquiry into the suspected offence** is being pursued with diligence and speed.

This protocol ensures that extensions to the standard custody time frame are not taken lightly and are justified by the necessity of further investigation while maintaining a commitment to conducting the inquiry efficiently and without undue delay.

2.2 Seeking Court Permission for Additional Detention

To detain a suspect beyond 36 hours, law enforcement must obtain authorisation from the Magistrates' Court through a warrant for further detention.

This legal mechanism allows for an extension of custody time, with the court capable of granting an additional 36 hours upon the first request, followed by a possible extension of 24 more hours upon a second request.

Consequently, the cumulative maximum duration a suspect can be held without charge is capped at 96 hours.

For the Magistrates' Court to approve such an extension, **several criteria** must be met:

(a) **The detainment must be related to allegations of an offence** that is either strictly indictable or triable.

(b) **There must be a justified belief that prolonging** the suspect's detention is critical for either safeguarding evidence that has yet to be secured, preserving existing evidence, or facilitating further interrogation that could yield significant evidentiary leads.

(c) **It must be evident that the ongoing investigation into the offence** is being pursued with diligence and efficiency, ensuring that any extension of detention is not a result of investigative delays but rather the complexity or scale of the investigation.

This process underscores the balance between the necessity of thorough investigation and the protection of indi vidual liberties, ensuring that extended detention is closely scrutinised and justified by the circumstances of the case.

3. Establishing Suspect Identification

The implementation of identification protocols is essential under **the following circumstances**:

(a) **A witness claims** to have recognised or suggests the possibility of recognising a suspect.

(b) **A witness asserts** they can identify a suspect from a prior encounter.

(c) There is a credible likelihood that an **eyewitness can positively identify the suspect** based on previous observations.

These protocols are intricately structured to assess the witness's ability to correctly identify the suspect as the same individual they observed earlier, aiming to prevent the occurrence of misidentification.

In scenarios where the suspect's identity is not established, the police might accompany the witness to the crime scene to facilitate an on-site identification. If this leads to the discovery and arrest of a suspect at the location, it is then obligatory to conduct a formal identification procedure. This step ensures the reliability of the witness's identification and secures its validity within the legal process.

Emma witnesses a theft at a local convenience store and reports seeing the perpetrator flee the scene. Based on her account and a general description of the suspect, the police initiate a search. Emma states she could recognise the thief if she saw them again.

Given Emma's confidence in her ability to identify the suspect, the police decide to use an identification procedure. They organise a video lineup, compiling footage of individuals who match the description provided by Emma, alongside the person they have under suspicion based on preliminary investigations.

Before conducting the video lineup, and since Emma mentioned the thief ran towards a nearby park, the police took her to the area to see if an on-the-spot identification was possible. This step is taken as there's a chance the suspect might still be in the vicinity and could be immediately recognisable to Emma.

As they arrive, Emma points out someone sitting on a bench who matches the thief's description. The police approach the individual and, after a brief investigation, detain them for further questioning.

Following the on-site identification and the suspect's detention, the police proceeded with a formal lineup to ensure the process adhered to legal standards and solidified the identification's credibility. Emma participates in this controlled environment, confirming her initial on-site identification.

This formal procedure helps reinforce the evidence against the suspect and safeguards against potential challenges to the identification's validity in court.

This scenario underscores the significance of conducting identification procedures meticulously to ensure the accuracy of witness identifications and protect the rights of suspects. The steps from the initial witness statement to the formal identification process highlight the balance between investigative needs and legal safeguards.

3.1 Suspects' Rights during Identification Process

During any identification procedure, suspects are entitled to several fundamental rights aimed at ensuring fairness and transparency throughout the process:

(a) **Explanation of the Procedure:** Suspects have the right to clearly explain the purpose and nature of the identification procedure, ensuring they understand what is happening and why.

(b) **Access to Legal Representation:** Suspects are entitled to seek legal advice free of charge and have the option of having a solicitor or a friend present during the procedure to provide essential support and guidance.

(c) **Understanding of Obligations and Consequences:** Suspects must be informed about their responsibilities and the potential implications of their actions, including:

- **Option to Decline Cooperation:** While suspects can choose not to participate in the procedure, they should be informed that the process might still proceed in their absence through covert means. Moreover, their lack of cooperation could be highlighted during any subsequent trial.

- **Impact of Altered Appearance:** Suspects should be aware that any significant changes to their appearance (such as shaving a beard, cutting hair, or altering their hairstyle) after being informed of the procedure could influence its execution. Such alterations might also be mentioned during a trial, potentially impacting the case's outcome.

These rights are designed to protect the integrity of the identification process and safeguard the suspect's legal interests, ensuring that the procedure is conducted in a just and equitable manner.

3.2 Identification Procedure Variants

The Police and Criminal Evidence Act 1984 (PACE), specifically in Code D, delineates four established methods for the identification of suspects, each designed to uphold the principles of accuracy and fairness in witness identification:

Video Identification:

This approach employs video sequences to display the suspect alongside at least eight similar individuals in age, stature, general appearance, and social status. The process is rigorously structured to ensure an equitable assessment by:

(a) It masks any distinct characteristics that could unfairly distinguish the suspect from the others in the lineup.

(b) Providing the suspect and their legal advisor an opportunity to express any legitimate concerns regarding the selection of the individuals included in the video lineup.

(c) Requiring that the video sequence is shown to the witness on at least two occasions, coupled with a caution that the lineup may not necessarily include the suspect.

(d) Isolate witnesses from each other if there are several to avoid any potential bias or influence on their identifications.

These measures are implemented to protect the validity of the identification process, reducing the likelihood of erroneous identifications while safeguarding the rights and integrity of the process for both suspects and witnesses.

Live Identification Parade:

This traditional method involves the physical assembly of the suspect alongside at least eight other individuals who share a resemblance in appearance.

This procedure is carefully managed to ensure fairness by:

(a) **Allowing** the suspect to voice objections regarding the setup or the individuals selected to stand in the lineup ensures a fair and unbiased process.

(b) **Giving** the suspect the autonomy to select their position in the lineup further enhances the impartiality of the identification process.

(c) **Informing** the witness before viewing the parade that the individual they are asked to identify might be absent among those lined up, setting a neutral expectation.

(d) **Ensuring** that, in cases involving multiple witnesses, each witness views the parade independently to prevent their observations from influencing one another.

(e) **Documenting** the parade through video recording or taking colour photographs serves as an objective record of the procedure for later review, if necessary.

These protocols aim to maximise the accuracy of witness identifications while protecting the rights of the suspect, ensuring the identification parade is conducted in a just and equitable manner.

Group Identification Procedure:

This method involves the witness observing the suspect within an informal setting among a group.

Key aspects of this procedure include:

(a) The **process** can proceed irrespective of the suspect's consent, although ethical considerations and the rights of the suspect are carefully weighed.

(b) The **choice of location** for this identification is critical. It should ensure that the individuals present resemble the suspect to some extent, avoiding any undue prominence of the suspect within the group.

(c) To **accurately document** the conditions under which the identification was made, a colour photograph or video recording of the group, including the moment of identification, should be captured immediately afterwards.

This approach aims to create a more natural context for identification, potentially reducing the pressure on the witness while still adhering to procedural fairness and the integrity of the identification process.

Confrontation Identification:

This less commonly used method involves a direct encounter between the witness and the suspect. Critical guidelines for conducting a confrontation identification include:

(a) **Informing** the witness beforehand that there is a possibility the individual they are asked to identify may be different from those presented during the confrontation, setting appropriate expectations.

(b) **Allowing** the presence of the suspect's solicitor or a chosen acquaintance, provided their attendance, does not introduce significant delays to the process.

(c) **Ensuring** the suspect is not physically restrained during the identification to maintain a neutral and non-coercive environment.

(d) Directly **asking** the witness if they recognise the suspect as the person they previously observed, with the question framed precisely: "Is this the person you saw on the earlier occasion?"

(e) **Given** its direct nature and the potential for stress on the witness, this procedure is rarely employed and typically conducted within the confines of a police station for control and safety.

The confrontation method is used with caution due to its potential impact on the witness and the suspect, ensuring it is reserved for situations where other forms of identification may not be feasible or have been inconclusive.

3.3 Challenges to Identification Evidence

Although the four identification methods outlined in Code D are legally sanctioned, video identification is the most frequently utilised. Challenges to the admissibility of video identification evidence might arise from the following:

(a) **Neglecting Reasonable Objections:** If the police fail to consider valid concerns about the similarity between the suspect and fillers in the lineup, the fairness of the procedure is compromised.

(b) **Improper Separation of Witness and Suspect:** Any failure to prevent the witness from seeing the suspect before or during the identification could prejudice the witness's impartiality.

(c) **Inadequate Isolation of Witnesses:** Failing to keep witnesses separated before or during the identification process can lead to contamination of their independent recollections.

(d) **Omission of Crucial Warnings to Witnesses:** Not informing witnesses of the possibility that the suspect may not be included in the lineup undermines the process's integrity.

3.4 Implications of Code D Violations

Violations of Code D protocols can have significant legal ramifications, potentially leading to the exclusion of identification evidence from trial. The court will assess whether including such evidence would detrimentally affect the trial's fairness to the extent that exclusion is justified.

This determination hinges on whether the procedural breach undermines the reliability of the identification or infringes upon the principles of justice, emphasising the critical importance of adhering to established guidelines during the identification process.

4. Establishing Suspect Identification

Interviewing a suspect during their detention at a police station is a standard investigative procedure. These interviews are conducted within a designated room and meticulously recorded to ensure the dialogue can be accurately referenced if the case advances to trial.

The recording process is **two fold**:

(a) **Audio and Video Documentation:** An audio recording of the interview is mandatory, with the option to capture video. This dual-mode recording aims to preserve the integrity of the verbal exchange.

(b) **Duplication for Security:** The practice involves creating two versions of the audio recording: a master copy, which is securely stored, and a working copy, which is used for review and analysis during the investigation and pre-trial preparations.

However, there are specific conditions under which a suspect should not be interviewed, including:

- **Cognitive Impairment or Intoxication:** If a suspect is deemed incapable of understanding the significance of the questions or their responses, or if they cannot grasp the proceedings due to intoxication or any other mental or physical condition, the interview should be postponed or suspended. This safeguard ensures that any information obtained during the interview is given knowingly and voluntarily, respecting the suspect's legal rights and the integrity of the investigative process.

These guidelines are designed to uphold the fairness of the interrogation process, ensuring that the evidence collected is both reliable and admissible while also protecting the rights and well-being of the suspect.

Interview with Audio and Video Recording:

Alex is detained on suspicion of committing fraud. Upon arrival at the police station, Alex is informed that an interview will be conducted in a room equipped with audio and video recording devices. The purpose is to ensure transparency and accuracy in documenting the proceedings. Alex is offered legal representation, and a solicitor is present throughout the interview.

During the interview, every question and response is captured on audio and video, with the conversation being simultaneously recorded onto two tapes - a master copy for official use and a working copy for immediate reference by the investigating team. This meticulous recording ensures that Alex's statements are accurately preserved for potential use in court, providing a clear and unbiased record of the interaction.

Suspect Under the Influence:

Jordan, suspected of vandalism, is visibly intoxicated at the time of arrest and detention. Recognising Jordan's condition, the duty officer decides to delay the interview. This decision is based on the understanding that Jordan's intoxication impairs his ability to comprehend the questions fully or to provide coherent and voluntary responses.

Instead, Jordan is allowed time to sober up, with the interview being rescheduled to ensure it can be conducted under conditions where Jordan is fully aware and capable of understanding the proceedings. This approach protects Jordan's rights and ensures the reliability and admissibility of the interview content in any subsequent legal proceedings.

These examples highlight the importance of adhering to procedural standards during police interviews, ensuring the suspect's rights are protected while maintaining the integrity and usefulness of the evidence collected.

4.1 Guidance for Suspects during Police Interview

A suspect's right to legal representation during a police interview is a cornerstone of the legal process, ensuring they are fully informed and supported when deciding how to engage with questioning.

A legal advisor's role in this context includes several key responsibilities:

(a) **Review of Custody Record:** The legal representative's first step is to examine the custody record meticulously. This document details every aspect of the suspect's detention, including times of arrest, imprisonment, and any interactions with police personnel. This review helps the legal advisor to understand the procedural context of the detainee's custody.

(b) **Securing Pre-Interview Disclosure:** Before the interview, the legal advisor will engage with the investigating officer to request disclosure regarding the case. While the police are not obligated to reveal all evidence to the legal advisor, they must share enough information to clarify the allegations against the suspect and the basis of their suspicion. This initial disclosure is crucial for the legal advisor to formulate appropriate advice, particularly regarding how the suspect should respond to police questioning.

The advice on whether a suspect should answer police questions is nuanced and must be tailored to the specific circumstances of each case. This decision is influenced by several factors, including the strength of the evidence disclosed, the nature of the allegations, and the potential legal implications of providing or withholding information during the interview. The advisor's objective is to protect the suspect's legal rights and interests, ensuring any decisions made about participating in the interview are informed and strategic.

Through these actions, the legal representative plays a pivotal role in safeguarding the suspect's rights and positioning within the legal process, ensuring they navigate the police interview with the benefit of comprehensive and informed legal advice.

4.2 Invoking the Right to Silence and Understanding the Caution

At the commencement of any police interview, a suspect will be formally cautioned, a statement outlining the suspect's rights during the interrogation. This caution is fundamental, ensuring the suspect is fully informed about their rights and the implications of their choices during the interview.

Key components of the caution include:

(a) **Right to Legal Representation:** The suspect is reminded of their entitlement to have a legal advisor present during the interview, reinforcing the importance of legal guidance throughout the questioning process.

(b) **Right to Silence:** The caution explicitly states that the suspect is not obligated to answer any questions. This right is crucial, allowing the suspect not to provide information that might inadvertently incriminate them.

(c) **Consequences of Statements Made:** The caution warns that anything the suspect says can be recorded and potentially used as evidence in court. This highlights the significance of each statement made during the interview and its impact on the case.

(d) **Adverse Inferences from Silence:** Importantly, the caution also includes a warning about the potential consequences of remaining silent on specific issues during the interview. If a suspect decides not to mention particular facts, which they later introduce in court, they may draw adverse inferences about the suspect's reasons for withholding this information initially. This aspect of caution underscores the strategic importance of deciding whether to speak or remain silent on particular matters during the interview.

Understanding the caution is essential for suspects, as it directly influences their approach to answering questions and managing their defence. It underscores the balance between protecting oneself from self-incrimination and the potential implications of withholding information pertinent to one's defence strategy in court.

Sam is detained by the police on suspicion of being involved in a burglary. Upon arrival at the police station, Sam is informed that legal representation is available and an interview will be conducted. Sam decides to wait for a solicitor before proceeding with the interview.

Before the interview begins, the interviewing officer presents Sam with the formal caution: "You do not have to say anything. But it may harm your defence if you do not mention something when questioned that you later rely on in court. Anything you do say may be given in evidence."

Sam's solicitor, after reviewing the custody record and obtaining preliminary disclosure from the police, advises Sam on the implications of the caution. Given the evidence disclosed, the solicitor suggests that Sam exercises the right to silence on specific questions, particularly those for which answering could potentially self-incriminate or where insufficient information is available to form a complete response.

Throughout the interview, Sam chooses to remain silent on several questions based on the solicitor's advice, mindful of the caution that their silence on specific matters could lead to adverse inferences in court. However, Sam and the solicitor have decided this approach is the best course of action given the circumstances.

At trial, the prosecution highlights Sam's refusal to answer specific questions during the police interview. Sam's defence explains the strategic reasons for remaining silent, emphasising that the decision was made with a clear understanding of the caution and with legal counsel. The court then considers whether it is appropriate to draw any adverse inferences from Sam's silence, taking into account the rationale provided and the context of the entire case.

This scenario demonstrates the careful consideration required when navigating the right to silence and understanding the caution in a police interview. It highlights the strategic decisions made by suspects and their legal representatives in balancing the need to protect against self-incrimination while mitigating the potential for adverse inferences in court.

4.3 Utilising the Special Caution

When it's pertinent to the investigation to explain the defendant's presence at the crime scene or to account for objects, substances, or marks found on them at the time of arrest, a more targeted approach is employed through particular caution. This caution is distinct in its application and prompts the defendant to explain specific evidentiary points that could significantly impact their defence if left unaddressed until trial.

The procedure for administering the particular caution includes the following:

(a) **Clarification of the Offence:** The officer conducting the interview must specify the offence under investigation to ensure the defendant understands the context and seriousness of the situation.

(b) **Detailing the Specific Fact in Question:** The suspect is then informed about the specific fact or evidence they are asked to explain. This could involve questioning their presence at a particular location, possessing certain items, or the origin of marks or substances found on their person.

(c) **Advisory on Adverse Inferences:** Importantly, the particular caution includes a warning that failing to explain during the interview, which the defendant later introduces in their defence in court, may lead to the court drawing adverse inferences. This is a critical juncture, as it highlights the potential legal ramifications of choosing to remain silent about critical aspects of the evidence against them.

This particular caution is designed to ensure that defendants are fully informed of the consequences of withholding information during police interviews, especially information that could be pivotal to their defence.

It underscores the delicate balance between exercising the right to silence and the strategic considerations of how this decision might be perceived in court, particularly about specific evidence directly implicating the defendant in the alleged crime.

Riley is arrested due to a series of burglaries in a residential neighbourhood. Upon arrest, officers find a unique tool in Riley's backpack that matches the description of a device used in the break-ins. During the initial phase of the police interview, the standard caution is given, and Riley opts to exercise the right to silence, answering only select questions with the guidance of a solicitor.

As the interview progresses, the focus shifts to the tool found in Riley's possession at the time of arrest. The interviewing officer issues a caution before questioning Riley about the tool. The officer clearly states the offence under investigation — burglary — and explicitly mentions the tool found with Riley, emphasising its significance to the case. Riley is then warned that failing to explain the presence of this tool now but later offering an explanation in court could lead to the court drawing adverse inferences about Riley's silence during the interview.

After a brief consultation with the solicitor, Riley decides to provide an account for the tool, explaining that it was borrowed from a friend for a wholly unrelated and legitimate purpose earlier that day, and Riley had forgotten it was in the backpack.

At trial, the prosecution highlights Riley's initial reluctance to discuss the tool during the early stages of the interview. However, Riley's defence points to the explanation provided after the particular caution was issued, arguing that it demonstrates a willingness to cooperate once the significance of the tool is made clear. The court then weighs the timing and nature of Riley's explanation in the context of the particular caution, considering whether the reason is credible and whether any adverse inferences should be drawn from the initial silence.

This scenario underscores the strategic importance of particular caution in the investigative process. It illustrates how the caution serves not only to protect the rights of the defendant by ensuring they are aware of the implications of their choices but also to aid in gathering potentially crucial information during the police interview. The decision to speak or remain silent, especially after a particular caution, can significantly impact how a defendant's actions are interpreted at trial.

4.4 Choices Available to the Suspect during Interview

During a police interview, a suspect has three strategic options regarding interacting with the questioning process. These options are designed to accommodate the suspect's right to a fair defence while allowing them to navigate the legal implications of their responses.

The options are as follows:

(a)   **Active Participation:** The suspect may choose to actively engage in the interview, answering the questions posed by the police. This approach allows the suspect to provide a comprehensive account of their side of the story, potentially clarifying misunderstandings or presenting information that could forgive them.

(b) **Choosing Silence:** Alternatively, a suspect can opt not to answer questions by verbally responding with "no comment" to inquiries or by choosing to remain completely silent. This strategy is often employed to avoid inadvertently providing information that could be misconstrued or used against them in court. However, suspects should be aware of the implications of the caution and how their silence might be interpreted, particularly in light of the particular caution regarding specific evidence or allegations.

(c) **Submission of a Written Statement:** The suspect has the right to submit a prepared written statement that outlines their account of the events in question. After submitting this statement, they can choose not to respond to further questions. This method allows the suspect to clearly articulate their position in a controlled manner, minimising the risk of misinterpretation during the live exchange of a verbal interview. However, it's crucial for the suspect and their legal advisor to carefully consider the content of this statement, as it will become a part of the official record and subject to scrutiny.

These options provide a framework for suspects to manage their legal risks while engaging in the police investigation process. The choice among these strategies should be made in consultation with legal counsel, considering the case's specifics, the evidence available, and the potential legal outcomes of each approach.

Taylor is arrested due to several thefts from a local shopping centre. Upon arrival at the police station, Taylor is informed of the right to legal representation and decides to wait for a solicitor before proceeding with the interview.

Option 1: Active Participation

Initially, Taylor and the solicitor decided that Taylor would actively participate in the interview to clarify certain misunderstandings. Taylor provides detailed answers to the police questions, explaining whereabouts during the times of the thefts and providing alibis. This proactive approach helps to clarify Taylor's non-involvement in the incidents.

Option 2: Choosing Silence

As the interview progresses, the police begin to question Taylor about a separate incident that Taylor does not know of. On the solicitor's advice, Taylor decides to respond with "no comment" to these questions. This decision is made to avoid any potential misinterpretation of Taylor's responses or inadvertently providing information that could complicate the situation further.

Option 3: Submission of a Written Statement

Before the interview concludes, the police will ask about Taylor's relationship with a known theft suspect. Taylor and the solicitor prepare a written statement overnight detailing Taylor's limited, casual acquaintance with the individual and lack of involvement in their criminal activities. The next day, Taylor handed in the statement at the start of the interview and then declined to answer further questions.

Aftermath

Taylor's strategic use of the available options during the interview—providing a complete account where beneficial, opting for silence when questions ventured into unfamiliar territory, and submitting a written statement on a complex issue—allowed for a nuanced approach to cooperating with the investigation while safeguarding personal legal interests.

This scenario demonstrates the importance of understanding and judiciously applying the options available during a police interview. With the guidance of legal counsel, suspects can navigate the interview process in a way that allows them to contribute to the investigation while minimising the risk of self-incrimination or misunderstanding.

4.5 Protections for Vulnerable Suspects

The Police and Criminal Evidence Act 1984 (PACE) establishes specific protections for vulnerable suspects, recognising their need for additional support during police procedures.

Vulnerable suspects include:

(a) **Youths**: Individuals under the age of 18.

(b) **Suspects with Mental Disorders or Other Vulnerabilities:** This includes those who may not fully understand the process or cannot communicate effectively during the interview.

Key Safeguards:

(a) **Identification of Vulnerability:** The custody officer must determine if a suspect is vulnerable at the outset of their detention, ensuring that additional protections are promptly implemented.

(b) **Access to an Appropriate Adult:** Vulnerable suspects have the right to the presence of an appropriate adult who can offer support and clarify the proceedings for them. An appropriate adult might be:

• The suspect's parent or guardian.

- A representative from a relevant care organisation.

- A social worker.

- A trained volunteer who is independent of the police force.

(c) **Presence During the Interview:** The appropriate adult must be present to provide emotional support, help with communication between the suspect and the interviewing officers, and ensure that the suspect's rights are upheld.

(d) **Respecting Suspect's Wishes:** When selecting an appropriate adult, the preferences of the suspect should be considered, adhering to the principle that the support provided should be in the suspect's best interest.

(e) **Impact on Evidence Admissibility:** Should there be a failure to involve an appropriate adult for a vulnerable suspect—inadvertently or otherwise—the legitimacy of any evidence gathered during the interview could be questioned. This could lead to the exclusion of such evidence under considerations related to the fairness of the trial, as outlined in later chapters on confessions and evidence exclusion.

These provisions underscore the justice system's commitment to fairness and the recognition that vulnerable individuals require specific considerations to participate meaningfully and safely in legal processes.

Jamie, a 16-year-old with diagnosed anxiety and difficulty in understanding complex situations, is brought into the police station on suspicion of vandalism. Recognising Jamie's age and condition, the custody officer immediately identifies Jamie as a vulnerable suspect.

Upon identification, the officer ensures an appropriate adult supports Jamie. Jamie expresses a preference for their guardian, Alex, to be present. The police contact Alex, who arrives at the station to act as Jamie's appropriate adult.

With Alex present, the police proceed to interview Jamie. Alex plays a crucial role, helping to explain the questions to Jamie in an understandable way and offering reassurance throughout the process. Alex also observes the interview to ensure that Jamie's rights are respected and that the interview does not exacerbate Jamie's anxiety.

Beyond mere presence, Alex actively ensures that the interview conditions are conducive to Jamie's participation. This includes requesting breaks when Jamie appears overwhelmed and clarifying legal terms or implications of the questions and Jamie's responses.

Despite Jamie's initial reluctance to discuss the incident, Alex's support enables Jamie to participate more fully in the interview process. Jamie explains their presence at the scene was coincidental and unrelated to the vandalism.

Later, in the proceedings related to the case, the court considers how Jamie's interview was conducted, including the presence and role of the appropriate adult. This consideration influences the court's view on the reliability and admissibility of Jamie's statements, ensuring the process respects Jamie's vulnerabilities.

This scenario underscores the importance of the safeguards PACE puts in place for vulnerable suspects, highlighting how the presence and intervention of an appropriate adult can significantly impact the fairness and effectiveness of the police interview process for young or vulnerable individuals.

4.6 Interview Methodology

Once a suspect is evaluated as competent for an interview—having received pertinent legal counsel and, where necessary, the accompaniment of an appropriate adult—the investigative team is positioned to commence the interview process.

Key steps and protocols include:

(a) **Recording Requirement:** The entirety of the interview must be documented to ensure an accurate and verifiable record of the exchange. Although audio recordings are standard, video recordings are increasingly utilised for their added layer of detail and context.

(b) **Issuance of the Caution:** At the interview's initiation, the suspect is presented with a caution to inform them of their rights and the potential implications of their choices during the interview. The standardised caution states:

(c) "You do not have to say anything, but it may harm your defence if you do not mention something you later rely on in court when questioned. **Anything you do say may be given in evidence.**"

This caution serves **multiple purposes**:

(a) **Right to Silence:** It reinforces the suspect's right not to engage in self-incrimination by choosing not to answer questions.

(b) **Consequence of Omission:** It highlights that failing to disclose information during the interview, later introduced in court, could potentially weaken the suspect's defence. This aspect underscores the strategic importance of deciding what information to share during the interview.

(c) **Use of Statements in Court:** It reminds the suspect that any statements made can be utilised as evidence, underscoring the need for careful consideration before speaking.

The procedure for conducting a police interview is meticulously designed to balance the investigation's needs with protecting the suspect's legal rights. This ensures that any evidence gathered through the interview process is obtained reasonably and can be reliably used in the judicial process.

4.7 Prohibition of Oppression and Inducement

To maintain the integrity of the police interview process and ensure compliance with legal standards, interviewing officers are bound by strict guidelines prohibiting the use of oppressive tactics and inducements.

These measures are vital for safeguarding the suspect's rights and ensuring that any information or confession obtained during the interview is voluntary and reliable.

Key principles include:

(a) **Oppression**: The definition of oppression encompasses actions that are torturous, inhuman, or degrading, including the actual or threatened use of violence. The interview environment should not intimidate or coerce the suspect into cooperating or confessing. This includes limiting the number of officers present during the interview to avoid creating an unnecessarily intimidating atmosphere.

(b) **Inducements**: Officers are expressly forbidden from offering inducements to the suspect in exchange for a confession. This prohibition includes suggesting that the suspect might receive a more lenient treatment, such as a police caution or eligibility for police bail, should they choose to confess. Such practices could undermine the voluntariness of the confession and lead to questions regarding its authenticity and admissibility in court.

(c) **Interview Environment:** The physical setting of the interview plays a crucial role in ensuring the suspect's comfort and willingness to participate. The room should be adequately heated, ventilated, and lit, creating conditions conducive to a fair and non-coercive interview process.

By adhering to these guidelines, the police aim to conduct interviews that respect the suspect's dignity and rights while preserving the credibility and admissibility of the evidence collected. These standards are designed to protect the suspect and uphold the integrity of the judicial process by ensuring that convictions are based on evidence obtained through lawful and ethical means.

4.8 Duties of a Solicitor during Detention

Under the Police and Criminal Evidence Act 1984 (PACE), a solicitor's role while present at a police station is explicitly focused on safeguarding and promoting their client's legal rights amidst the police investigation.

This encompasses a range of responsibilities to ensure the suspect's treatment aligns with legal standards and that their rights are fully protected.

Critical aspects of the solicitor's role include:

(a) **Rights Protection:** Ensuring the police respect all the suspect's rights under PACE. This involves thoroughly understanding these rights and vigilance in their application throughout the detention and interview process.

(b) **Disclosure Acquisition:** Part of the solicitor's role involves obtaining as much information as possible from the police regarding the nature of the accusations against their client and the evidence supporting them. This disclosure is critical for the solicitor to provide informed advice to the suspect.

(c)   **Advisory on Questioning:** The solicitor advises the suspect on approaching police questioning. This advice may sometimes lead to the suspect withholding certain information that could inadvertently bolster the prosecution's case. The solicitor must balance protecting the suspect's rights with the legal implications of withholding information.

(d)   **Intervention Rights:** During the interview, the solicitor has the right to intervene for several reasons, including:

  •   **Seeking Clarification:** If a question is ambiguous or confusing, the solicitor can request clarification to ensure their client fully understands what is being asked.

  •   **Challenging Questioning Practices**: The solicitor may challenge any questions or interviewing tactics deemed improper or coercive.

  •   **Advising Against Answering:** If a question poses a risk to the suspect's legal position, the solicitor may advise the client not to answer.

  •   **Requesting Breaks:** The solicitor can ask for the interview to be paused to provide additional legal advice to the suspect, ensuring they are fully informed before continuing.

The solicitor's presence and active participation during the police interview are crucial in balancing the police's investigative needs and the suspect's legal rights, ensuring the suspect does not inadvertently compromise their legal defence. This role underscores the importance of legal representation in criminal justice, providing a necessary check on police procedures and safeguarding the suspect's rights.

Lena, a 25-year-old graphic designer, is arrested during a high-profile cybercrime investigation. Upon her detention, Lena exercises her right to legal representation, and Solicitor Smith is assigned to her case.

Solicitor Smith immediately reviews Lena's custody record upon arrival at the police station. He ensures that Lena understands her rights under PACE and confirms that these rights have been respected since her detention.

Smith meets with the investigating officers to obtain disclosure about the allegations against Lena and the evidence they have gathered. The officers provide general details about the cybercrime investigation but are reluctant to share specific proof. Smith insists on receiving sufficient information to advise Lena properly, highlighting the importance of transparency for a fair legal process.

Based on the information received, Smith advises Lena on approaching the upcoming interview. He suggests that Lena answer questions about her whereabouts during the times in question but recommends saying "no comment" to technical questions about the cybercrime, given the complexity of the allegations and the potential for misinterpretation.

During the Interview:

(a)   When the police ask Lena about her expertise in specific software alleged to be used in the crime, Smith intervenes to seek clarification on how this line of questioning relates to Lena's specific involvement.

(b)   At one point, an officer's questioning becomes aggressive, and Smith challenges the manner, reminding the officer of the need for a respectful and non-coercive interview environment.

(c)   Smith requests a pause in the interview to discuss a new piece of evidence presented by the police, ensuring Lena fully understands its implications before responding.

The careful navigation of the interview, with Smith's interventions and advice, allows Lena to provide helpful information without compromising her defence. His presence ensures that the police adhere to proper procedure and that Lena's rights are protected throughout the process.

This scenario exemplifies the multifaceted role of a solicitor during a suspect's detention and police interview. By advocating for Lena's rights, obtaining and reacting to disclosure, advising on answering questions, and intervening when necessary, Solicitor Smith plays a crucial role in ensuring the integrity of the legal process and protecting Lena's interests.

4.9 Avoiding Professional Misconduct during Interviews

Strict professional standards govern the conduct of solicitors during police interviews to ensure that their presence supports the legal process without impeding the police investigation.

While a solicitor's primary duty is to protect their client's rights, there are clear boundaries that must not be crossed:

(a) **Non-Obstruction:** A solicitor must refrain from obstructing the interview process. Acts of obstruction could include coaching the suspect on how to respond to questions or speaking on behalf of the suspect during the interview. Such actions undermine the interview's integrity and contradict the ethical standards expected of legal professionals.

(b) **Consequences of Obstruction:** Should solicitors engage in obstructive behaviour, they risk being removed from the interview room to prevent further interference with the investigation. This drastic measure requires authorisation from a police superintendent and is employed only in exceptional circumstances, reflecting its rarity and the seriousness with which it is regarded.

(c) **Rights Following Removal:** If a solicitor is removed for obstructing an interview, the suspect retains the right to consult with another solicitor. This ensures that the suspect's right to legal representation is preserved, regardless of any misconduct by their initially chosen solicitor.

The solicitor conduct guidelines at the police station are designed to maintain a balance between facilitating a suspect's legal defence and ensuring the lawful and effective gathering of evidence. By adhering to these standards, solicitors contribute to the fairness and efficacy of the criminal justice process while safeguarding their clients' rights and interests.

Marcus, a 30-year-old suspected of embezzlement, is brought in for questioning. Marcus's solicitor, Mr Green, accompanied him to ensure his legal rights were upheld during the interview.

As the interview progresses, Mr. Green becomes overly protective of Marcus. When the police ask Marcus about specific financial transactions, Mr. Green interjects, suggesting phrases Marcus could use to deny involvement. On several occasions, Mr Green answers questions directed at Marcus, citing complex legal defences.

The interviewing officers warn Mr Green about his obstructive behaviour, emphasising the need for Marcus to speak for himself. Despite the warnings, Mr Green continues to intervene inappropriately.

Seeing no improvement, the lead officer contacts a superintendent to report the situation. After a brief review, the superintendent authorises Mr. Green's removal from the interview room to prevent further obstruction of the investigation.

Marcus is visibly distressed by the turn of events. The police paused the interview, allowing Marcus time to consult with another solicitor from the same legal firm who was on standby. This new solicitor, Ms Patel, adheres to the professional standards expected, facilitating the interview process without interfering.

Following the incident, Mr Green faces a review by the legal and regulatory body for his conduct, highlighting the importance of professional integrity and the non-obstructive role of solicitors during police interviews.

This scenario demonstrates the delicate balance solicitors must maintain between advocating for their client's rights and respecting the procedural requirements of police interviews. It underscores the importance of professional conduct in the legal process and the mechanisms in place to address misconduct, ensuring that the rights of the suspect and the integrity of the investigation are preserved.

4.10 Decision-Making on Police Bail Post-Charge

After a suspect is formally charged with an offence, the next critical decision involves determining the conditions of their custody pending a court appearance.

This decision falls to the custody officer at the police station and hinges on whether the charged individual should be:

(a) **Remanded in Custody:** The suspect is detained at a police or correctional facility until they can be presented in court.

(b) **Released on Police Bail:** The suspect is released from custody under specific conditions, with a mandate to appear in court at a later, designated date.

Involvement of the Defence Representative:

Before making this decision, the custody officer will consider submissions from the suspect's defence representative. This input can include arguments for the suspect's release on bail, emphasising factors such as the suspect's community ties, lack of flight risk, and any other mitigating circumstances that support their release pending trial.

Criteria for Bail Consideration:

The custody officer's decision to grant police bail mirrors the considerations applicable to court bail, as detailed in subsequent chapters.

These factors include:

(a) The **nature and seriousness** of the alleged offence.

(b) The **strength of the evidence** against the suspect.

(c) The **suspect's character,** antecedents, associations, and community ties.

(d) The **suspect's past compliance** or non-compliance with bail conditions.

(e) The **risk of the suspect** failing to appear in court, committing further offences while on bail, or interfering with witnesses or the course of justice.

This process ensures that the decision to remand a suspect in custody or release them on bail is made with due consideration of both the suspect's rights and the public interest. The custody officer's role in this decision underscores the balance between ensuring the accused's appearance at trial and upholding the principle of liberty before conviction.

CHAPTER 3. BAIL APPLICATIONS IN COURT

1. Steps for Requesting Bail

When a defendant finds their request for bail denied by the police, the subsequent step involves appearing before the Magistrates' Court at the earliest scheduled session.

While the bail hearing lacks a fixed protocol, it typically unfolds as follows:

(a) **Presentation of Objections by the Prosecution:** Should there be any reservations regarding granting bail, it is standard for the prosecution to detail these concerns initially. This might include risks of the defendant absconding, potential interference with witnesses, or the likelihood of reoffending.

(b) **Defence's Counterarguments and Bail Conditions Proposal:** Following the prosecution, the defence can argue in favour of granting bail, addressing the prosecution's objections. The defence may suggest specific bail conditions to mitigate perceived risks, such as residence requirements, electronic tagging, or restrictions on contacting particular individuals.

Relaxation of Evidence Rules:

The evidentiary standards during bail hearings are notably more lenient than those at trial. This flexibility acknowledges that the entire collection and formal submission of evidence still need to be completed at this stage. Occasionally, witnesses may be called upon to substantiate specific claims relevant to the bail application, like verifying a proposed bail address.

Issuance of a Certificate of Full Argument:

Should the court decide against granting bail, or if it chooses to impose specific conditions on the bail, it must articulate its reasoning publicly. When bail is denied, the defendant receives a certificate of the entire argument. This document confirms that the court thoroughly considered the bail application arguments before it decided to refuse, ensuring a transparent and accountable decision-making process regarding bail.

2. Entitlement to Bail

The decision-making process regarding the remand status of a defendant during adjournments is a critical aspect of pre-trial proceedings.

This process entails determining whether to:

(a) **Remand in Custody:** This outcome means the defendant will be detained in a correctional facility until their next court appearance.

(b) **Remand on Bail:** Alternatively, the defendant may be released from custody pending their next court hearing, with the expectation that they will present themselves at court on the specified date. Bail may be imposed with specific conditions or granted unconditionally.

General Right to Bail:

Defendants typically possess a fundamental right to be granted bail. This principle supports the presumption of innocence until proven guilty and the notion that unnecessary pre-trial detention should be avoided.

Criteria for Custodial Remand:

The court is only justified in ordering a defendant to be remanded in custody if:

(a) **An Exception to Bail Rights is Applicable:** Certain circumstances, such as the risk of the defendant fleeing, committing further offences, interfering with witnesses, or the severity of the crime, may warrant a deviation from the general right to bail.

(b) **Likelihood of Custodial Sentence Upon Conviction:** The court must also consider the probability of imposing a prison sentence if the defendant is found guilty. This assessment reflects the seriousness with which the court views the allegations and the potential risk to public safety or the judicial process.

This framework ensures that the decision to deny bail and remand a defendant in custody is not taken lightly, balancing the need to protect society and the integrity of the legal process against the individual rights and freedoms of the defendant.

3. Criteria Limiting Bail Eligibility

The general presumption of granting bail is counterbalanced by specific conditions under which bail may be justifiably withheld.

These conditions are designed to address potential risks associated with releasing a defendant before trial. Bail may be denied in instances where there is a considerable likelihood that the defendant would:

(a) **Not Comply with Court Appearances:** Evidence or indications suggest the defendant might not attend future court hearings.

(b) **Engage in Additional Criminal Activities:** Concerns exist over the possibility of the defendant committing new offences while out on bail.

(c) **Tamper with Evidence or Influence Witnesses:** Potential actions by the defendant could undermine the fairness of the trial process.

Furthermore, specific scenarios necessitate a cautious approach to granting bail:

(a) **Serious Offences with Prior Bail:** Defendants facing charges for grave offences triable in the Crown Court, such as GBH, mainly if they were previously granted bail for a different matter when the alleged crime occurred.

(b) **Safety of the Defendant:** Circumstances where remaining in custody are considered safer for the defendant.

(c) **Potential Harm to Others:** Significant reasons to believe the defendant, if released on bail, might pose a risk of causing physical or psychological harm to someone with whom they have a close relationship.

(d) **Ongoing Imprisonment:** Defendants who are already serving sentences for other convictions.

(e) **Insufficient Information for a Bail Decision:** The court needs more details to decide on bail responsibly.

(f) **History of Non-Compliance or Bail Violations:** Defendants who have previously failed to adhere to court schedules or breached conditions set during the current legal proceedings.

By delineating these exceptions, the legal framework aims to judiciously weigh the rights of individuals against the potential threats to public safety, the welfare of specific individuals, and the sanctity of the judicial process, ensuring that bail decisions are made with thorough consideration of all pertinent factors.

Evaluating Substantial Grounds for All Decisions:

When assessing whether substantial grounds exist to justify either the granting or denial of bail, the court meticulously evaluates criteria to ensure a balanced decision.

These **criteria** include:

(a) **Nature and Seriousness of the Offence:** The court examines the gravity of the charged offence and anticipates the likely sentence or penalty, considering whether it would lean towards custody, a community order, or a fine. More severe charges often skew towards a stricter stance on bail.

(b) **Character and History of the Defendant:** This encompasses assessing the defendant's past behaviour, including any previous convictions, which might indicate a pattern of disregard for the law. Conversely, a lack of prior offences, strong community bonds, and affiliations with reputable organisations can bolster the defendant's case for bail, suggesting a lower flight risk and a commitment to adhering to bail conditions.

(c) **Bail Compliance Record:** The defendant's history of complying with previous bail conditions is scrutinised to gauge their reliability and the likelihood of adherence to future bail terms.

(d) **Evidence Strength:** The probative value of the evidence against the defendant is a critical factor. Strong evidence suggests guilt can influence the court's decision to deny bail based on the assumption that a defendant might abscond or interfere with the judicial process if the likelihood of conviction is high.

(e) **Potential Risk to Others:** The court considers any indications that the defendant, if released, could pose a risk of causing harm, either physically or mentally, to others. This assessment is particularly relevant in cases involving allegations of violence, harassment, or threats.

These considerations are integral to the judicial process, providing a comprehensive framework for courts to determine bail applications. By taking into account the severity of the offence, the defendant's background, their adherence to previous bail conditions, the weight of the evidence, and the potential risk to public safety, the court aims to make decisions that balance the rights of the defendant with the interests of justice and community safety.

4. Implementing Conditions on Bail

Courts can impose specific, tailored conditions on bail to mitigate potential risks while allowing defendants conditional freedom. These conditions ensure public safety, prevent further offences, and guarantee the defendant's future court appearances.

Conditions are set based on their relevance to the case, their proportionality to the offence and the defendant's circumstances, and their practical enforceability.

Commonly applied bail conditions include:

(a) **Residency Requirement:** To ensure stability and monitorability, the court may stipulate that the defendant must reside at a predetermined address, which could be with a family member or in a designated bail hostel.

(b) **Police Station Reporting:** Defendants might be required to report to a local police station regularly, facilitating a check on their whereabouts and compliance with bail conditions.

(c) **Area Restrictions:** To reduce the risk of reoffending or interfering with the investigation, a defendant may be prohibited from entering specific areas, particularly those related to the offence or where potential witnesses reside.

(d) **No-Contact Orders:** Directives preventing the defendant from contacting specific individuals, such as victims, co-defendants, or witnesses, help to protect the integrity of the judicial process and the safety of those involved.

(e) **Curfew Implementation:** Setting a curfew restricts the defendant's movements during certain hours, typically overnight, aiming to reduce the opportunity for reoffending.

(f) **Electronic Monitoring:** Electronic tags allow authorities to monitor the defendant's compliance with curfew or geographic restrictions.

(g) **Surety Requirement:** A guarantee from a surety (a third party) may be demanded, which is forfeited if the defendant fails to comply with the bail conditions, especially the requirement to surrender to court. This adds a level of financial accountability to the bail agreement.

These conditions are not exhaustive and can be combined or customised to address the specific concerns raised by each case. The imposition of bail conditions reflects the court's effort to balance the defendant's rights with the need to protect the community and ensure the smooth progression of the legal process.

5. Bail Considerations for Murder Charges

When dealing with bail applications in murder cases, the legal framework imposes stringent criteria, significantly altering the standard presumption towards granting bail.

In such instances, the responsibility for hearing bail requests falls exclusively to a Crown Court Judge, and the inclination shifts decidedly against the defendant's release. The underlying principle for this shift is the high risk associated with the severity of the charge.

Accordingly, bail may only be considered if the court is convinced that the defendant does not pose a significant risk of committing any further offences that could result in physical or mental harm to others.

6. Subsequent Bail Applications

The court is obligated to reassess the bail status of a defendant at every hearing. Despite this ongoing review, a defendant is typically restricted to making just one additional bail application based on the same grounds and evidence previously presented. This limitation prevents the court system from being burdened with repetitive requests that do not introduce new arguments or evidence.

However, the rules allow for flexibility in certain circumstances: A defendant can submit further bail applications if there has been a material change in their situation. This can include the emergence of new evidence that undermines the prosecution's case or a change in the defendant's circumstances, such as securing a new, more stable bail address.

This framework ensures that while the court maintains a consistent approach to bail considerations, there remains an avenue for defendants to argue for their release on bail if significant new factors come into play that could reasonably affect the court's decision.

7. Consequences of Bail Violations

The integrity of the bail system relies heavily on the defendant's compliance with set conditions and their commitment to appear in court as required.

Breaches of bail conditions and failure to surrender as per the bail agreement carry significant legal repercussions:

(a) **Immediate Arrest for Breach:** A defendant found violating any condition of their bail can be arrested without needing a warrant. This immediate consequence underscores the importance of adhering to the conditions set forth by the court.

(b) **Bail Withdrawal or Stricter Conditions:** Following a breach, the court can either revoke the defendant's bail entirely or impose more severe conditions to mitigate any further risk of non-compliance. This may include stricter curfews, additional reporting requirements, or more restrictive movement limitations.

(c) **The offence for Failing to Surrender:** Not appearing in court as required by bail conditions constitutes a separate criminal offence. This act of absconding undermines the judicial process and compounds the defendant's legal challenges, introducing new charges that could lead to further penalties.

(d) **Increased Risk of Bail Revocation:** Disregarding bail conditions or court orders significantly increases the likelihood of revoking bail. The court's decision to grant bail is predicated on trust in the defendant's compliance; thus, any breach erodes this trust and justifies reconsidering the defendant's suitability for bail.

These measures are in place to ensure that defendants on bail remain accountable for their actions while awaiting trial, protecting the community and maintaining the efficacy and credibility of the judicial system.

CHAPTER 4. INITIAL APPEARANCES IN MAGISTRATES' COURT

1. Commencement of Criminal Prosecutions

The Magistrates' Court serves as the initial venue for most criminal cases in England and Wales, where individuals aged 18 or older charged with any criminal offence make their first court appearance.

The nature of this initial hearing varies significantly based on the category of offence with which the defendant is charged:

These are less severe crimes, such as minor assault or battery. At this stage, the defendant is asked to plead or not guilty.

(a) **Guilty Pleas:** Should the defendant admit to the offence, the court may proceed directly to sentencing unless there is a need for pre-sentence reports to inform the decision.

(b) **Not Guilty Pleas:** In cases where the defendant denies the charges, the court will schedule a trial date, typically six to eight weeks later, and issue directions concerning the exchange of evidence (disclosure) between the prosecution and defence.

Either way, Offences include theft or criminal damage, where the court undertakes a 'plea before venue' procedure. This process involves initially determining how the defendant wishes to plead and then deciding whether the case should be tried in the Magistrates' Court or referred to the Crown Court based on factors such as the seriousness of the offence and the court's sentencing powers.

Serious crimes such as rape, robbery, or murder fall into this category. These offences bypass the preliminary hearing in the Magistrates' Court and are directly referred to the Crown Court for trial, given their complexity and the severity of potential sentences.

This structured approach ensures that each case is allocated to the court most appropriate for its nature and severity, allowing for an efficient and effective judicial process.

2. Functions of the Defence Solicitor

At the outset of the legal proceedings within the Magistrates' Court, the defence solicitor plays a pivotal role in ensuring the defendant's rights are protected and that they are entirely prepared for the initial hearing.

Securing Disclosure from the Prosecution:

The defence solicitor is tasked with obtaining crucial information from the prosecution that outlines the evidence against the defendant.

This process of securing disclosure is essential for:

(a) **Preparing the Defence:** Enabling the solicitor to formulate a robust defence strategy by understanding the prosecution's case.

(b) **Representation Order:** If a representation order, which authorises legal aid for the defendant, is in place, the solicitor can request disclosure before the first court appearance. This ensures the defence team has adequate time to review the prosecution's evidence and plan accordingly.

(c) **Variability Based on Offence Type:**

- **Indictable Only Offences:** Given these cases are destined for the Crown Court, initial disclosure at the Magistrates' Court level is minimal, primarily focusing on confirming the charge and proceeding to transfer.

- **Summary Only and Either Way Offences:** The extent of disclosure depends on the defendant's custodial status before the first court appearance. Defendants produced from custody may quickly receive a basic summary of the offence and any prior convictions. More detailed information, including interview outlines, witness statements, and any victims' impact statements, might be provided if appearing on bail.

This early disclosure stage is critical for setting the groundwork of the defence, allowing the solicitor to advise the defendant accurately on plea considerations and to prepare for the initial hearing comprehensively.

Gathering Client Instructions:

An essential aspect of preparing for the first court appearance involves the defence solicitor obtaining comprehensive instructions from the defendant.

This process includes:

(a) **Analysing Prosecution Disclosure:** The solicitor reviews the evidence provided by the prosecution with the defendant, gauging their reaction to witness statements and other disclosed materials.

(b) **Preliminary Account from the Defendant:** Although time constraints at court may limit the ability to gather a complete statement, the solicitor aims to secure a concise yet thorough account of the defendant's version of events and their perspective on the prosecution's evidence.

This initial gathering of instructions is pivotal for shaping the defence strategy and advising the defendant accurately on how to proceed.

Maintaining Professional Ethics:
The solicitor's role is underpinned by a dual obligation to zealously represent the client's interests while upholding the integrity of the legal system.

This balance requires:

(a) **Advancing the Client's Interests:** The solicitor strives to protect and promote the defendant's legal rights, working within the legal framework to achieve the best possible outcome.

(b) **Upholding Court Honesty:** The solicitor must ensure their advocacy does not involve indirectly deceiving the court. This includes the accurate presentation of the defendant's case and evidence.

(c) **Navigating Conflicts:** When a solicitor's duty to the court and the duty to their client clash, the solicitor must carefully advise the defendant on the implications of their decisions. If an irresolvable ethical dilemma arises, the solicitor may need to consider withdrawing from representing the client to maintain professional integrity.

These principles guide the solicitor in providing effective legal representation while adhering to the ethical standards of the legal profession, ensuring that the defence strategy respects both the client's interests and the justice system's requirements.

Emma is charged with theft from her employer and makes her first court appearance at the Magistrates' Court. Her defence solicitor, Mr Patel, obtains the prosecution's initial disclosure, which includes witness statements and CCTV footage allegedly showing Emma stealing goods.

Upon reviewing the prosecution's evidence with Emma, Mr Patel noted discrepancies in the witness statements and areas where the CCTV footage was unclear. Emma insists she is innocent and identifies a possible misinterpretation of the CCTV evidence. She also points out that one of the witnesses may hold a personal grudge against her, potentially biasing their statement.

Mr Patel quickly but thoroughly documents Emma's responses, ensuring he understands her account and her views on the evidence against her. This information is crucial for challenging the prosecution's case and planning the defence strategy.

As the case progresses, Emma suggests to Mr Patel that she could claim to have been elsewhere during the theft, proposing they find someone to corroborate this false alibi. Here, Mr Patel faces an ethical dilemma: while he must champion Emma's defence, he cannot condone or facilitate misleading the court.

Mr Patel explains to Emma the importance of honesty in her defence, particularly the potential consequences of presenting false evidence. He highlights his duty not to mislead the court and advises Emma that pursuing a false alibi could severely damage her case and lead to additional charges.

Feeling the weight of Mr. Patel's advice, Emma reconsiders and agrees to focus on the inconsistencies and potential bias in the prosecution's evidence rather than fabricating an alibi.

In court, Mr Patel effectively challenged the credibility of the witness statements and highlighted the ambiguity in the CCTV footage without compromising his ethical obligations. The Magistrates find the evidence against Emma insufficient for a conviction, leading to her acquittal.

This scenario underscores the defence solicitor's role in meticulously preparing a client's case, the importance of clear communication between the solicitor and client, and the ethical boundaries within which solicitors operate.

By navigating these aspects judiciously, Mr Patel ensures Emma's right to a fair defence is upheld while maintaining the integrity of the legal process.

Providing Comprehensive Advice to the Client:

A defence solicitor's guidance is instrumental in navigating the complexities of the legal system and making informed decisions.

After obtaining and reviewing the client's instructions, the solicitor advises on several critical aspects:

(a) **Evaluating the Prosecution's Evidence:** The solicitor assesses the strengths and weaknesses of the prosecution's case against the defendant. This evaluation includes an analysis of the evidence's reliability, the credibility of witnesses, and any legal or factual challenges that can be raised. Based on the current evidence, the goal is to provide the defendant with a realistic understanding of the likelihood of conviction.

(b) **Sentencing Prospects and Plea Benefits:** Understanding the potential consequences if convicted is crucial for the defendant's decision-making. The solicitor explains the range of possible sentences, considering the specific offence and the defendant's circumstances. Notably, the solicitor outlines the benefits of an early guilty plea, which can lead to a reduced sentence under the principles of credit for early guilty pleas, emphasising the importance of this consideration in the decision to plead guilty or not guilty.

(c) **Case Preparation Strategies:** The solicitor identifies the steps necessary to build a robust defence, including gathering additional evidence and securing witness statements or expert testimonies. This preparation is tailored to counter the prosecution's case and support the defendant's version of events.

(d) **Choice of Trial Court for Either-Way Offences:** A trial at the Magistrates' Court or the Crown Court is significant for defendants charged with either-way offences. The solicitor explains each option's procedural differences, potential outcomes, and strategic considerations. This includes discussing the Magistrates' Court's more limited sentencing powers versus the Crown Court's jury trial but higher potential penalties, helping the defendant to make an informed choice about where to face trial.

This advisory process ensures that the defendant is well-informed about their legal situation, understands the implications of various decisions, and is prepared to navigate the court proceedings effectively.

In advising a client on their plea, it is paramount for a defence solicitor to maintain a role that respects the defendant's autonomy while providing expert legal advice. Key principles include:

(a) **Autonomy in Plea Decisions:** The ultimate decision to plead guilty or not guilty rests solely with the defendant. A solicitor's role is to inform and advise, not to dictate the course of action the defendant should take. This ensures that the defendant's legal rights and personal agency are preserved throughout the legal process.

(b) **Informative Guidance on Evidence:** A critical aspect of the solicitor's advice involves candidly assessing the prosecution's evidence against the defendant. This includes highlighting the case's strengths and advising the defendant when the evidence appears compelling. Such transparency is crucial for the defendant to make an informed decision about their plea.

(c) **Advising on Sentencing Implications:** The solicitor should clearly explain the potential sentencing outcomes for both guilty and not guilty pleas. This includes discussing the concept of credit for an early guilty plea, which can lead to a reduced sentence. The defendant should understand the tangible benefits of this option and the potential consequences of proceeding to trial with a strong case against them.

(d) **Empowering the Defendant's Decision-Making:** While the solicitor provides a detailed analysis of the evidence, potential sentencing outcomes, and procedural considerations, it is imperative that the defendant feels supported to make their own decision regarding the plea. The solicitor's advice should empower the defendant, giving them the knowledge and understanding to navigate their options effectively.

This approach ensures that the defendant is fully informed about their legal situation, understands the implications of various plea decisions, and is supported in making the most appropriate choice.

3. Securing a Representation Order

For defendants not privately financing their defence, securing a representation order becomes a necessary step undertaken by the defence solicitor to ensure legal representation in court.

The application for such an order is made to the court handling the defendant's case. To be eligible for a representation order, the defendant must meet two critical criteria:

(a) **The Interests of Justice Test:** This assessment determines whether granting legal representation is essential for a fair hearing, considering factors such as the complexity of the case, the potential for a custodial sentence, and any difficulties the defendant may have in presenting their case due to lack of legal knowledge, age, mental health, or other vulnerabilities.

(b) **The Means Test:** This evaluation examines the defendant's financial situation to ascertain whether they possess the means to afford private legal representation. The test considers the defendant's income, assets, and living expenses to ensure that state-funded legal assistance is provided to those who genuinely need it.

Successfully passing both these tests confirms the defendant's entitlement to legal aid through a representation order, facilitating access to necessary legal support without financial burden.

3.1 Criteria under the Interests of Justice Test

For allocating a representation order under the legal aid scheme, the interests of justice test evaluates several factors to determine the necessity of legal representation for ensuring a fair trial. These factors include:

(a) **Risk of Severe Consequences:** The likelihood of the defendant facing significant adverse outcomes, such as imprisonment, loss of employment, or substantial damage to reputation, is a primary consideration. The offence's gravity, specifics, and the defendant's prior character and societal contributions are assessed. The potential severity of the offence is judged based on the prosecution's arguments, including the implications of existing suspended sentences or community orders, which may heighten the risk of a custodial sentence.

(b) **Legal Complexity:** Cases that are expected to delve into intricate legal issues, such as disputes over legal principles, the admissibility of complex evidence like identification, hearsay, or the implications of silence, are likely to warrant the granting of legal aid. The necessity for legal expertise in navigating these areas underscores the importance of representation.

(c) **Defendant's Ability to Engage with the Process:** Factors such as the defendant's age, comprehension of the English language, or other vulnerabilities that may impair their understanding of the proceedings or ability to articulate their defence are critically evaluated. This ensures that all defendants can participate fully and fairly in their defence, regardless of personal circumstances.

(d) **Necessity for Investigative Work:** The requirement for specialised legal tasks, such as locating and interviewing witnesses or expert cross-examination, indicates the need for professional legal representation. Cases demanding technical or forensic analysis or where the evidence requires rigorous scrutiny highlight the importance of legal assistance.

(e) **Benefit to Others:** In instances where the outcome of the case holds significant implications for other individuals, such as cases involving allegations of sexual or violent offences where the testimony of the complainant may be subject to cross-examination, the provision of legal representation ensures that the proceedings are conducted with the necessary sensitivity and expertise.

These considerations are integral to the legal aid decision-making process, ensuring that defendants facing proceedings that could profoundly impact their lives, involve complex legal questions, or require a level of procedural engagement beyond their capability are afforded the necessary legal support to ensure justice is served.

3.2 The Means Test for Legal Aid

The allocation of a representation order, in addition to satisfying the interests of justice criteria, requires passing the means test designed to assess the financial eligibility of the defendant for legal aid. This test ensures that state-funded legal assistance is provided to those who cannot afford private legal representation.

The **criteria** include:

(a) **Automatic Qualification:** Defendants under the age of 18 or those receiving certain types of government support, such as income support, income-based Jobseeker's Allowance, state pension, or income-related Employment and Support Allowance, are automatically deemed eligible for legal aid without the need for further financial scrutiny.

(b) **Income Threshold for Eligibility:** Defendants who do not fall into the automatically qualified categories must demonstrate that their financial means are below a specific threshold to qualify for legal aid. The current (December 2023) eligibility threshold is set at £3,398 of annual disposable income or capital and/or equity below a threshold of £30,000. This figure represents the defendant's net income after necessary deductions, such as taxes and living expenses, have been accounted for. Defendants are required to substantiate their financial status through the submission of relevant financial documents.

(c) **Assessment Process:** The means test involves a detailed examination of the defendant's income, expenditures, and financial obligations to determine their disposable income. This assessment ensures that legal aid is allocated relatively, prioritising assistance to those most in need while maintaining the integrity of the legal aid system.

Defendants whose adjusted annual income exceeds the £3,398 threshold or capital and/or equity below a threshold of £30,000 may need to explore alternative avenues for legal representation or consider partial contributions towards their defence costs if their income is marginally above the limit. This financial eligibility criterion is critical to the legal aid process, aligning resource allocation with the principles of need and fairness.

CHAPTER 5. PLEA BEFORE VENUE PROCEDURES

1. Steps Involved when a Defendant Pleads

When a defendant is charged with an offence categorised as 'either way', meaning it can be tried in either the Magistrates' Court or the Crown Court, they undergo the procedure known as a plea before the venue.

This procedure ensures the defendant makes an informed decision regarding their plea and the venue for their trial.

The key steps include the following:

(a) **Presentation of the Charge:** The specific charges against the defendant are formally presented, clarifying the nature of the either way offence(s) they face.

(b) **Initial Plea:** The defendant is asked for their initial plea to the charge(s). This plea does not determine the final venue but initiates the process of venue selection based on the defendant's indication of guilt or innocence.

(c) **Venue Selection Discussion:** Following an initial plea of not guilty, or if the defendant desires to contest the charges, a discussion occurs regarding the most suitable venue for the trial.

2. Guiding the Defendant on Choice of Venue

An integral component of the defence solicitor's role in the plea before venue process is to provide comprehensive advice on selecting the trial venue.

This advice should encompass:

(a) **Advantages of Magistrates' Court:** The defence solicitor outlines the benefits of electing for a trial at the Magistrates' Court, which may include a faster resolution of the case, potentially lower legal costs, and the perception of more lenient sentencing for certain offences compared to the Crown Court.

(b) **Advantages of Crown Court Trial:** Conversely, the solicitor explains the benefits of choosing a Crown Court trial, such as the presence of a jury, which some defendants prefer for a fair hearing, especially in complex cases or those involving serious allegations. The Crown Court is also perceived to have broader sentencing powers, which can be advantageous in cases where the defendant might seek a more nuanced consideration of mitigating factors.

(c) **Disadvantages and Risks:** The solicitor should discuss each option's potential disadvantages and risks. For example, while a Crown Court trial offers the benefit of a jury, it may also involve longer waiting times for a trial date and the possibility of more severe sentences if convicted.

This advice is crucial for enabling the defendant to make an informed decision about their trial venue, balancing the strategic advantages against each option's personal and legal implications.

2.1 Benefits of Opting for Magistrates' Court

Choosing the Magistrates' Court for trial offers several distinct advantages for defendants charged with either way offences:

(a) **Limited Sentencing Powers:** One of the primary benefits is the Magistrates' Court's restricted ability to impose sentences, capped at six months' imprisonment for a single offence. This limitation can be particularly appealing for defendants facing charges that, in the Crown Court, might result in longer sentences.

(b) **Efficiency and Cost-Effectiveness:** Trials in the Magistrates' Court are generally faster and less costly than those in the Crown Court. This expedites the legal process and potentially reduces the financial burden on the defendant, especially concerning contributions towards legal costs in the event of a conviction.

(c) **Simplified Disclosure Requirements:** The procedural obligations for the defence are less demanding in the Magistrates' Court. Notably, submitting a defence case statement is optional, alleviating some of the preparatory workload and strategic disclosure considerations facing the defence team.

2.2 Advantages of Selecting Crown Court

Conversely, opting for a Crown Court trial carries its own set of benefits:

(a) **Higher Acquittal Rates:** Historical data suggests that the Crown Court has a higher rate of acquittals than the Magistrates' Court. This statistic can influence defendants who believe a jury trial offers a better chance of a not-guilty verdict.

(b) **Robust Evidence Challenges:** The Crown Court provides a more formal and comprehensive framework for contesting the admissibility of evidence. This environment can be advantageous for cases where the defence will challenge prosecution evidence, potentially without a jury rigorously.

(c) **Extended Preparation Time:** The longer time-frame before a Crown Court trial can benefit the defence's case preparation. This delay allows for more thorough evidence gathering, witness preparation, and overall strategic planning, which can be crucial for complex or evidence-heavy cases.

These advantages highlight the strategic considerations that defendants and their legal representatives must evaluate when deciding on the trial venue for either offence. The choice between the Magistrates' Court and the Crown Court involves balancing the immediate practicalities of the legal process against the broader tactical approaches to securing the most favourable outcome.

3. Determining the Appropriate Court for Trial

When a defendant intends to plead not guilty or does not specify a plea for an either-way offence, the Magistrates' Court is tasked with deciding the most suitable venue for the trial.

This decision-making process, known as allocation, involves a careful assessment of **several factors:**

(a) **Defendant's Criminal Record:** The court examines the defendant's prior convictions to gauge the severity of the current charges within the context of the defendant's criminal history. This assessment helps determine if the pattern of offending or the nature of past convictions suggests a need for potentially more extraordinary sentencing powers available in the Crown Court.

(b) **Sentencing Powers of the Court:** A critical consideration is whether the Magistrates' Court's sentencing capabilities sufficiently address the offence(s) in question. This includes evaluating the court's maximum sentencing authority for a single offence and its aggregate power for multiple charges in light of the sentencing guidelines. The court assesses if its potential penalties align with the offence's seriousness and the defendant's conduct.

(c) **Arguments from Defence and Prosecution:** Both parties can present their views regarding the most appropriate trial venue. This includes discussions on whether the Magistrates' Court's sentencing powers are adequate for the case and any legal or practical reasons favouring one venue.

Should the Magistrates' Court conclude that its sentencing powers are insufficient or that the complexity or seriousness of the case warrants it, the decision will be made to transfer the case to the Crown Court. This ensures that the trial is conducted in a court equipped with the appropriate authority and resources to deal justly and effectively.

4. Choosing the Trial Venue

Upon the Magistrates' Court agreeing that it has the capacity (jurisdiction) to handle the case, the choice of trial venue is presented to the defendant.

This stage is critical for determining the course of the trial based on the defendant's preferences:

(a) **Option for Summary Trial:** The court informs the defendant that the trial can proceed within the Magistrates' Court. At this juncture, the defendant either agrees to a trial in the Magistrates' Court or opts for a trial in the Crown Court. The defendant is advised that even if they agree to a summary trial and are found guilty, the case might still be escalated to the Crown Court for sentencing, especially if the Magistrates' Court deems its sentencing powers inadequate.

(b) **Setting a Trial Date:** If the defendant consents to a summary trial, a date for the trial is scheduled in the Magistrates' Court. This expedites the legal process, potentially leading to a quicker resolution.

(c) **Electing Crown Court Trial:** Should the defendant choose not to undergo a summary trial, the case is immediately transferred to the Crown Court. This decision may be influenced by the defendant's desire for a jury trial or a perception of a more favourable outcome in the higher court.

4.1 Requesting a Sentencing Indication

Before making a plea, the defendant can request from the Magistrates' Court an indication of whether the likely sentence, should they plead guilty, would involve custody. This request is aimed at informing the defendant's decision regarding their plea.

It's important to note that the court is not mandated to provide such an indication. If it chooses to offer guidance and the defendant subsequently pleads guilty based on this indication, the court is generally expected to adhere to the indicated sentencing approach.

If, after receiving a sentencing indication, the defendant decides to maintain a not-guilty plea and is later found guilty, the court is not bound by any sentencing indication previously given. This allows the court flexibility in sentencing based on the trial's outcome.

These procedures underscore the importance of informed decision-making by the defendant regarding their plea and the trial venue, facilitated by legal advice and, where available, indications from the court on potential sentencing outcomes.

5. Procedure for Low Value Theft Cases

In the legal framework for handling theft charges, a nuanced approach is applied to cases of low-value theft—specifically, theft where the value involved does not exceed £200.

This category of theft is subject to a hybrid procedural model that blends elements of both summary and either-way offences:

(a) **Mandatory Jurisdiction of Magistrates' Court:** Unlike typical either-way offences where the Magistrates' Court has the discretion to either retain the case or refer it to the Crown Court based on its assessment of the adequacy of sentencing powers, low-value theft cases are automatically deemed within the jurisdiction of the Magistrates' Court. This means the court is compelled to hear these cases and cannot refuse based on the offence's perceived seriousness or complexity.

(b) **Defendant's Right to Elect Trial Venue:** Despite being treated as summary offences in terms of jurisdiction, defendants charged with low-value theft retain the right to choose their trial venue. They may consent to have their case heard and decided in the Magistrates' Court or elect for a trial in the Crown Court, where a jury would determine their guilt or innocence.

This hybrid approach ensures that while low-value theft cases are streamlined through the Magistrates' Court to expedite justice and reduce the burden on higher courts, defendants do not lose their fundamental right to opt for a jury trial in the Crown Court if they believe it is in their best interest. This method balances the need for efficient case handling with preserving defendants' rights to a fair trial process.

Alex is accused of stealing electronics valued at £150 from a local store. Given the theft's value, the case falls under the category of low-value theft and is initially handled as a summary-only offence due to its valuation not exceeding £200.

The charge is presented as a low-value theft upon Alex's first appearance in the Magistrates' Court. The court explains to Alex that, despite the offence being treated as a summary-only matter for jurisdiction purposes, Alex retains the option to conduct the trial in the Crown Court.

Alex's defence solicitor outlines the advantages and disadvantages of hearing the case in the Magistrates' Court versus the Crown Court. The solicitor explains that the Magistrates' Court is likely to handle the case more swiftly and with potentially lower legal costs but also informs Alex of the right to a jury trial in the Crown Court, which some defendants prefer for a variety of reasons, including the perception of a fairer trial process.

After considering the solicitor's advice, Alex opts for a summary trial in the Magistrates' Court, valuing the speed of resolution and the lower complexity of the proceedings. Alex appreciates the straightforward nature of the case and feels confident in the evidence supporting a not-guilty plea.

The trial proceeds in the Magistrates' Court, where Alex is found not guilty based on compelling evidence that the alleged theft did not occur as charged. The decision to keep the case in the Magistrates' Court facilitated a quicker resolution, allowing Alex to resume daily life without the extended delay of a Crown Court trial.

This scenario demonstrates the unique hybrid approach to low-value theft cases, ensuring efficient legal processing while preserving the defendant's right to choose their trial venue. It underscores the importance of informed decision-making, guided by legal counsel, in navigating the judicial system.

6. Direct Transfer to Crown Court without Allocation

In certain circumstances, cases involving either way offences bypass the typical plea before venue and allocation process, being directly sent to the Crown Court.

This direct transfer occurs under specific conditions:

(a) Charges Including Indictable Only Offences: When a defendant, or any co-defendant, faces charges that combine an either-way offence with an indictable only offence, and both charges are presented simultaneously, the case must be escalated to the Crown Court. This requirement ensures that all related charges are tried in the appropriate court, reflecting the seriousness of the indictable-only offence. Should the either way offence and the indictable only offence be brought up on separate occasions, there remains the possibility, though not the certainty, of the case being sent to the Crown Court.

(b) Severe or Complex Fraud Cases: The prosecution may identify certain cases as serious or complex, especially those involving fraud. In these instances, the prosecution can request that the case be moved directly to the Crown Court, where the trial procedures and available resources are better suited to handle the intricacies and specifics of such cases.

(c)   Protection of Child Witnesses: In cases involving child cruelty or specific sexual offences where child witnesses are involved, the prosecution may advise that the welfare of these witnesses would be better served in the Crown Court setting. This considera- tion prioritises the sensitive handling of cases in- volving minors, ensuring that the trial environment is conducive to their protection and well-being.

These exceptions to the standard plea procedure before venue and allocation highlight the legal system's adaptab- ility in addressing some instances' unique needs and complexities. By allowing direct transfer to the Crown Court under these conditions, the judicial process ensures that cases are tried in a venue equipped to handle their specific requirements and sensitivities.

CHAPTER 6. PRE-TRIAL ORGANISATION IN THE MAGISTRATES' COURT

1. Efficient Preparation for Summary Trials

A systematic case management approach is adopted in the preparatory stages, leading to a summary trial within the Magistrates' Court.

This procedure follows the plea's conclusion before venue decisions for either offence opting for summary trial or immediately after a summary-only offence receives a not guilty plea. This regimen enhances the trial's efficiency through meticulous planning and collaboration.

Essential components of this pre-trial organisation include:

(a) **Scheduling Witness Testimonies:** The prosecution and defence outline their intended witness lists, ensuring all necessary evidence is presented and accounted for in the trial's timeline.

(b) **Streamlining Prosecution Evidence:** An agreement is reached on the prosecution witnesses whose statements will be admitted as read, thus narrowing the trial's focus to key disputed evidence and conserving valuable court time.

(c)   **Trial Duration Forecast:** An estimate is provided for the expected trial duration, considering the case's complexity and the volume of evidence, which facilitates optimal court planning.

(d)   **Anticipating Legal Requests:** By identifying potential legal applications beforehand, such as requests for evidence exclusion, the court can better anticipate and accommodate these legal discussions, contributing to a fluid trial process.

(e)   **Special Arrangement Identification:** Recognising any unique trial requirements early on, such as the need for interpreters or specific witness accommodations, ensures that all participants can effectively engage with the trial.

(f)   **Incentivising Early Plea Discussions:** Verifying that defendants are informed about the sentencing benefits of an early guilty plea encourages case resolutions where guilt is accepted, promoting judicial efficiency.

(g)   **Reinforcing Trial Attendance:** Ensuring defendants are aware that the trial will proceed in their absence highlights the significance of their active participation in the judicial process.

Adopting this structured pre-trial organisation, the Magistrates' Court actively directs the groundwork for the upcoming trial, aiming to reduce delays and ensure a streamlined, equitable proceeding. This proactive stance on case management reflects a commitment to maintaining the judicial process's effectiveness and integrity.

2. Setting Case Management Directions

Following the establishment of a framework for trial preparation, the Magistrates' Court issues specific directives to ensure the prosecution and defence are adequately prepared for the upcoming trial.

These guidelines, designed to streamline the pre-trial process, include the following:

(a) **Evidence and Notices by the Prosecution:** The prosecution must submit all its evidence to the defence, along with any notices regarding the intention to present lousy character evidence, within 28 days. This ensures the defence has sufficient time to review and respond to the materials presented.

(b) **Defence Statement and Witness Requirements:** The defence must submit a defence statement, should one be necessary, within 14 days. Additionally, the defence must notify the court and prosecution within seven days which of the prosecution's witnesses they wish to have present for cross-examination. Any objections to the prosecution's flawed character evidence must also be indicated within these seven days.

(c) **Notice of Defence Evidence:** The defence should notify the court and prosecution within 14 days if they intend to introduce hearsay evidence or evidence about the bad character of prosecution witnesses. Furthermore, statements from defence witnesses who will not be called to testify must be submitted within this timeframe to allow for a comprehensive understanding of the defence's case.

(d) **Legal Points of Contention:** Any legal issues, particularly those concerning the admissibility of critical pieces of evidence like identification, interview records, or confessions, should be raised at least 21 days before the trial. This advanced notice provides adequate time for legal arguments to be prepared and heard, minimising delays during the trial.

(e) **Certificates of Readiness:** Both parties must submit readiness certificates at least seven days before the trial, confirming their preparedness for the proceedings. This final check ensures that all pre-trial directions have been complied with and that the case can proceed smoothly.

These case management directions serve as a roadmap for the timely and orderly preparation for trial, emphasising the importance of adherence to deadlines and the efficient exchange of information between the prosecution and defence. The court facilitates a fair and reasonable trial process by setting these clear expectations.

3. Scheduling Preliminary Hearings

For cases classified as indictable only and thus directly referred to the Crown Court, preliminary hearings are scheduled to ensure the efficient progression of the case.

These hearings are convened within 14 days of the case's transfer to the Crown Court under specific circumstances, such as:

(a) **Extended Trial Duration:** If the anticipated trial duration exceeds four weeks, a preliminary hearing is set to discuss the logistical and scheduling challenges of longer trials.

(b) **Case Management Concerns:** Preliminary hearings address case management issues that could complicate the trial process, ensuring that procedural and substantive matters are resolved efficiently.

(c) **Requirement for an Early Trial Date:** In situations where there is a pressing need for the trial to commence at the earliest possible date, whether due to the nature of the case or external factors, a preliminary hearing helps expedite the trial schedule.

(d) **Involvement of Young Defendants:** Cases involving defendants under 18 are given priority, with preliminary hearings scheduled to consider the specific needs and legal protections afforded to juvenile participants in the criminal justice system.

(e) **Anticipation of an Early Guilty Plea:** When there is an indication that a defendant may enter an early guilty plea, a preliminary hearing allows the court to prepare for the plea and potentially for sentencing, streamlining the process for both the court and the defendant.

These preliminary hearings play a critical role in the Crown Court's pre-trial organisation, allowing for the early identification and resolution of any issues that could affect the trial's timing or conduct. By addressing these matters proactively, the court ensures that the trial can proceed as smoothly and efficiently as possible.

4. Conducting Plea and Trial Preparation Hearings

In the Crown Court, the plea and trial preparation hearing (PTPH) represents a crucial step in the pre-trial phase, occurring 28 days following the transfer of the case from the Magistrates' Court. This hearing will streamline the trial process by clarifying the charges and the defendant's responses.

Critical aspects of the PTPH include:

(a) **Arraignment of the Defendant:** This is the formal process during the PTPH, where the defendant is asked to enter their plea to the charges listed in the indictment. It is a critical moment that determines the course of the case, whether it will proceed to trial or move towards sentencing based on the plea.

(b) **Negotiation on Charges:** In some instances, to streamline the case and focus on the most pertinent charges, the prosecution may opt to 'offer no evidence' on specific counts in exchange for the defendant's guilty plea on others. This negotiation can lead to a more efficient resolution of the case, focusing resources and court time on the most significant aspects of the alleged criminal conduct.

(c) **Counts Lying on the Court File:** Another outcome of plea negotiations may be for some counts to 'lie on the court file', implying that the prosecution will not actively pursue these charges but remain on record. Like the offer of no evidence, this approach allows the legal process to concentrate on the core issues at hand, with the understanding that the unresolved counts could theoretically be reactivated under certain conditions, although this is rare.

These procedural steps during the PTPH are instrumental in defining the path forward for the case, facilitating a focused and efficient approach to trial preparation or moving directly to sentencing where applicable. The hearing ensures that all parties are aligned on the charges being contested and establishes a clear framework for the subsequent phases of the judicial process.

4.1 Procedure Following a Guilty Plea

Upon a defendant's guilty plea in the Crown Court, the next step involves moving towards sentencing. Before entering a guilty plea, a defendant can request a sentencing indication from the judge, known as a Goodyear indication.

This gives the defendant a clearer understanding of the potential sentence, facilitating an informed decision regarding their plea. Should the judge provide such an indication and the defendant plead guilty, the judge is committed to adhering to the indicated sentencing parameters.

4.2 Handling a not Guilty Plea

Conversely, the court focuses on trial preparation if the defendant enters a not-guilty plea. The judge will engage with counsel to establish a comprehensive overview of the case, which includes:

(a) **Case Facts and Logistics:** Counsel is required to present an outline of the case, including critical facts and the logistical aspects of the trial, such as the number of witnesses, their availability, and any requirements for special measures to facilitate their testimony (e.g., video links, screens for anonymity).

(b) **Defence Case Statement Issues:** The judge will inquire into any concerns stemming from the defence case statement, ensuring clarity and addressing any potential legal complications early in the process.

(c) **Evidential and Legal Matters:** Discussion extends to the sufficiency of the prosecution's evidence, the necessity for expert testimony, and the admissibility of hearsay and flawed character evidence. These dialogues are pivotal in identifying and resolving evidentiary issues that could impact the trial's conduct.

(d) **Additional Legal Considerations:** Any other relevant legal issues are reviewed, ensuring that all aspects of the case are thoroughly examined before setting a trial date.

This meticulous approach to managing a not-guilty plea ensures that all parties are adequately prepared for the trial, with a clear understanding of the case's complexities and logistical requirements. The Crown Court aims to proactively facilitate a fair, efficient, and effective trial process by addressing these elements.

5. Obligations for Evidence Disclosure by the Prosecution

The prosecution's responsibilities regarding evidence disclosure are pivotal in ensuring a fair trial. These duties, governed by strict timelines and legal principles, include:

(a) **Disclosure Timeline:** The prosecution is allocated a timeframe of 50 days to complete disclosure proceedings if the defendant is in custody, which extends to 70 days if the defendant has been granted bail. This period ensures the defence has adequate time to review the prosecution's evidence and prepare their case.

(b) **Evidence Disclosure:** The core of the prosecution's duty involves disclosing all evidence it plans to use at trial. This encompasses any testimony, physical evidence, or documents the prosecution will present to establish the defendant's guilt.

(c) **Unused Material Disclosure:** Beyond the evidence presented at trial, the prosecution must disclose any unused material that could undermine the prosecution's case or assist the defence. This includes evidence that might cast doubt on the reliability of prosecution witnesses, suggest an alternative narrative, or otherwise be favourable to the defendant's case. The principle behind this duty is to maintain the integrity of the judicial process by ensuring that all potentially exculpatory or relevant material is made available for the defence's consideration.

(d) **Ongoing Duty:** The obligation to disclose is not static; it is a continuous duty that requires the prosecution to reassess and disclose additional material that emerges as relevant before or during the trial. This ensures the defence can access all material evidence throughout the legal proceedings.

(e) **Handling Sensitive Material:** In cases where the prosecution possesses sensitive material that, if disclosed, could jeopardise public interest, national security, or intelligence operations, a specific protocol is followed. The prosecution must request a court hearing in chambers to argue for the non-disclosure of such material on the grounds of public interest immunity (PII). These hearings allow the court to balance the need to protect sensitive information against the defendant's right to a fair trial.

By adhering to these principles of evidence disclosure, the prosecution fulfils its legal and ethical obligations, contributing to the fairness and integrity of the criminal justice process.

Sam is charged with serious fraud and is awaiting trial in the Crown Court. Due to the case's complexity, Sam has been granted bail, setting the prosecution's disclosure deadline at 70 days.

Within the stipulated timeframe, the prosecution discloses all evidence it intends to rely on during the trial. This includes financial records, witness statements attesting to Sam's involvement in the fraud, and correspondence allegedly implicating Sam in the fraudulent activities.

The prosecution also reviews additional material gathered during the investigation, which includes statements from employees who vouched for Sam's integrity and questioned the evidence's interpretation. Recognising that this material could assist Sam's defence by offering an alternative explanation or casting doubt on the prosecution's narrative, the prosecution discloses this unused material to Sam's defence team.

Two weeks before the trial, further investigation uncovers emails that suggest a misunderstanding might have led to the fraudulent activities being misattributed to Sam. The prosecution, adhering to its ongoing duty of disclosure, promptly provides this new evidence to the defence.

The case also involves financial data that, if disclosed, could compromise ongoing intelligence operations. The prosecution applies to a PII hearing, requesting the court to permit withholding this sensitive material from open court proceedings to protect national security. After reviewing the material in chambers, the judge agrees that specific documents will be withheld on PII grounds but ensures that this decision does not prejudice Sam's right to a fair trial.

Armed with the full spectrum of disclosed evidence, including the recently uncovered emails, Sam's defence team successfully challenges the prosecution's case. The additional unused material and the careful consideration of PII issues ensure that the trial is conducted fairly, respecting both the public interest and the defendant's legal rights.

This scenario demonstrates the critical role of the prosecution's duty of disclosure in the justice system, ensuring that all relevant evidence, whether supporting the prosecution or the defence, is considered. It highlights the balance between transparency and protecting sensitive information, ensuring a fair trial process.

CHAPTER 7. EVIDENCE ADMISSIBILITY AND BURDEN OF PROOF

1. Establishing Guilt in Court

In criminal proceedings, the foundational principle of justice mandates that the prosecution establishes the defendant's guilt. This principle is encapsulated in the burden of proof, which rests squarely on the shoulders of the prosecution.

The essence of this responsibility and its implications include:

(a) **Prosecution's Obligation:** The prosecution is tasked with proving beyond a reasonable doubt that the defendant committed the offence(s) they are charged with. This high standard is central to ensuring fairness in the legal process, safeguarding against the wrongful conviction of innocent individuals.

(b) **Standard of Proof:** The "beyond reasonable doubt" threshold is the highest standard of proof required in any legal proceeding. It compels the judge (in the Magistrates' Court) or jury (in the Crown Court) to reach a level of conviction where they are firmly convinced of the defendant's guilt based on the evidence presented.

(c) **Defendant's Rights:** Consistent with the presumption of innocence, the defendant is not required to prove their innocence. Instead, the onus is on the prosecution to build a compelling case that leaves no room for reasonable doubt regarding the defendant's guilt.

(d) **Impact of Reasonable Doubt:** Should the defence successfully introduce a reasonable doubt about any critical element of the charged offence, the defendant is entitled to an acquittal. It's important to note that an acquittal does not equate to a declaration of innocence but indicates that the prosecution has failed to meet the requisite standard of proof.

(e) **Acquittal Implications:** An acquittal signifies that the court is not sufficiently convinced of the defendant's guilt to justify a conviction under the law. This outcome underscores the legal system's commitment to erring caution, prioritising that a guilty person should be more accessible than an innocent person to be wrongfully convicted.

This framework for the burden and standard of proof serves as a cornerstone of criminal justice, ensuring that the process of determining guilt is rigorous and fair and upholds the accused's fundamental rights.

2. Handling Visual Identification Evidence

Visual identification evidence, where a witness recounts the appearance or identifies the perpetrator they observed during the commission of a crime, poses significant challenges due to its inherent unreliability.

Despite the best intentions and sincerity of witnesses, the risk of misidentification remains a critical concern, primarily because honest witnesses can, and often do, make mistakes in identification. Factors such as stress, lighting conditions, the witness's vantage point, and the time elapsed since the event can all contribute to inaccuracies.

To mitigate the risk of misidentification and ensure the fairness of the identification process:

(a) **Identification Procedures:** When there is potential contention regarding the offender's identity, law enforcement agencies must conduct a formal identification procedure. This is essential in cases where the defendant disputes being at the crime scene or participating in the offence.

(b) **Video Identification Parade:** The most common method employed is the parade. This involves presenting the witness with a video lineup of individuals who match the general physical description of the suspect, including the accused. The lineup is carefully constructed to avoid suggesting who the suspect might be, reducing the possibility of influencing the witness's decision.

(c) **Procedure for Witness Identification:** During the video identification parade, the witness is asked if they can recognise the offender among the individuals shown in the video. This method aims to recreate the conditions under which the witness observed the suspect, albeit in a controlled environment, to gauge the accuracy of their memory and perception.

The careful handling of visual identification evidence is crucial in the judicial process, recognising the delicate balance between leveraging eyewitness accounts and safeguarding against wrongful convictions due to misidentification. By adhering to standardised identification procedures, the criminal justice system strives to uphold the integrity of trials and protect the rights of those accused.

2.1 Applying the Turnbull Guidelines

In cases where a witness's identification of a suspect is a central element, especially when the defence contests such evidence, the court must apply the Turnbull guidelines.

These guidelines are criteria established to assess the reliability and strength of visual identification evidence. To facilitate the recollection and application of these guidelines, the mnemonic **ADVOCATE** is often used, with each letter representing a crucial factor to be considered:

(a) **A - Amount of Time:** The duration for which the witness observed the suspect, as more prolonged exposure may enhance the reliability of their identification.

(b) **D - Distance:** The proximity between the witness and the suspect at the time of the observation, as a closer distance could lead to a more accurate identification.

(c) **V - Visibility:** The clarity and lighting conditions under which the witness saw the suspect influence the precision of their observation.

(d) **O - Obstruction:** The presence of any barriers or obstacles that might have impeded the witness's

view, potentially affecting the accuracy of their identification.

(e) **K - Known or Unknown:** Familiarity can significantly impact recognition if the suspect was previously known to the witness.

(f) **A - Any Reason to Remember:** Specific reasons
why the witness would particularly remember the
suspect, such as distinctive features or behaviours.

(g) **T - Time Lapse:** The period between the incident
and the identification procedure, with shorter inter-
vals generally leading to more reliable identifications.

(h) **E - Errors:** Any initial inaccuracies or errors in the
witness's description of the suspect, which might cast
doubt on their subsequent identification.

Applying these guidelines is crucial in ensuring that identification evidence is scrutinised for reliability before being presented to the jury or bench. By methodically applying these factors, the court safeguards against wrongful
convictions based on misidentification, maintaining the
integrity of the judicial process.

2.2 Judicial Assessment of Identification Evidence

The assessment of identification evidence is a critical judicial responsibility, mainly when such evidence is the primary basis for the prosecution's case.

The judge's determination regarding the strength of this evidence has significant implications for the trial's progression:

(a) **Weak Identification without Corroboration:** If the judge deems the identification evidence inherently weak—lacking in reliability and without any supporting evidence—the appropriate action is to remove the decision from the jury's hands. In such instances, the judge will direct an acquittal, concluding that the evidence presented is insufficient to support a conviction beyond a reasonable doubt.

(b) **Sufficient Strength or Corroborative Support:** Conversely, should the judge ascertain that the identification evidence possesses sufficient credibility, or if additional evidence exists that corroborates a weak identification, the matter is left to the jury's discretion. In this scenario, the jury must evaluate the evidence's integrity and determine whether it meets the standard of proof required for a conviction.

(c) **Defence Strategies in Trial:** If the case is put before the jury during the trial, the defence can rigorously scrutinise the identification evidence through cross-examination. Utilising the ADVOCATE mnemonic, the defence can systematically challenge the witness's testimony, highlighting potential weaknesses or inconsistencies in the identification process. By questioning the witness on the amount of time they observed the suspect, the distance of the observation, visibility conditions, any possible obstructions, and so forth, the defence seeks to cast reasonable doubt on the reliability of the witness's identification.

This careful evaluation of visual identification evidence by both the judge and the defence is vital to safeguard against the miscarriage of justice, ensuring that convictions are based upon thoroughly vetted evidence and found to be robust and credible.

Jordan is on trial for burglary, with the primary evidence against him being the identification of a neighbour who claims to have seen Jordan near the crime scene. The neighbour's testimony is the cornerstone of the prosecution's case, but the defence contends that the identification is unreliable.

During the trial, it becomes apparent that the neighbour only saw the suspect briefly at night and from a distance. There are no other witnesses, and the physical evidence found at the scene is inconclusive and does not directly link Jordan to the crime.

The judge reviews the identification evidence against the Turnbull guidelines and concludes that the evidence is weak and lacks corroborative support. The neighbour's testimony under cross-examination reveals inconsistencies, and they admit to not wearing their glasses at the time of the observation.

Given the frailty of the identification and the absence of supporting evidence, the judge decides to withdraw the case from the jury, directing an acquittal. The judge determines that the evidence presented does not meet the standard required to convict safely.

Jordan is acquitted based on the judge's direction, emphasising the importance of robust identification evidence in criminal proceedings. The scenario highlights judges' critical role in safeguarding against wrongful convictions based on unreliable witness testimony.

This example demonstrates how a judge may assess the strength of identification evidence and the circumstances under which a case may be withdrawn from the jury to prevent a potential miscarriage of justice.

2.3 Instructing the Jury on Identification Evidence Caution

At the close of a trial involving identification evidence, it is incumbent upon the presiding judge to deliver a specific caution to the jury, known as the Turnbull warning. This directive is designed to underscore the care with which the jury must approach the witness identification testimony.

Key elements of the Turnbull warning include:

(a) **Cautionary Principle:** The judge must emphasise the necessity for particular caution when considering identification evidence. The jury should be reminded that even confident witnesses can be mistaken, and the risk of misidentification increases when corroborative witnesses are mistaken.

(b) **Assessment of Witness Observation:** The jury is invited to scrutinise the conditions under which the identification was made. This involves reflecting on the witness's opportunity for precise observation, the duration of the sighting, and any other pertinent factors that could impact the reliability of the identification.

(c) **Highlighting Identification Flaws:** Any specific weaknesses in the identification evidence should be pointed out to the jury. In conjunction with the mnemonic ADVOKATE, the judge should guide the jury to consider factors such as the duration and quality of the observation, any obstructions, lighting conditions, and the witness's prior knowledge of the suspect, among others:

A - amount of time under observation;
D - distance between witness and suspect/incident;
V - visibility including time of day and lighting;
O - obstructions blocking the view;
K - known suspect from before;
A - any reason to remember the suspect;
T - time lapse between first and later identification;
E - errors or discrepancies.

By delivering the Turnbull warning, the judge ensures that the jury is fully aware of the potential pitfalls of identification evidence and the importance of a measured and critical evaluation of such testimony before reaching a verdict. This procedural safeguard is a vital aspect of the trial process, helping to prevent wrongful convictions based on unreliable eyewitness identification.

3. Consequences of Defendant Silence

The defendant's right to silence is fundamental in criminal justice, yet its exercise during investigation or trial carries potential implications.

While a defendant is never compelled to speak or present a case, choosing not to provide information at specific junctures can lead to certain presumptions by the court:

(a) **Adverse Inferences:** Should a defendant elect to remain silent during questioning or not offer an explanation for evidence that suggests their involvement in a crime, the court may infer that their silence indicates an acknowledgement of guilt or lack of a credible defence.

(b) **Impact on the Defence:** The decision to remain silent, especially in incriminating circumstances, can weaken the defendant's position. It may suggest to the jury or judge that there is no satisfactory response to the allegations, reinforcing the prosecution's case.

(c) **Insufficiency for Conviction:** It is crucial to understand that adverse inferences alone cannot serve as the sole basis for conviction. There must be substantial evidence establishing guilt beyond a reasonable doubt. Inferences drawn from silence are supplementary, potentially tipping the scales when the evidence is equivocal but insufficient to meet the burden of proof required for conviction.

This nuanced approach to the defendant's silence ensures that while the prosecution can highlight the lack of response as potentially indicative, the core of a conviction must always rest on the strength of the evidence presented against the defendant. The capacity to draw adverse inferences from silence is a balancing factor in assessing the defendant's stance in light of the evidence.

Criteria for Adverse Inferences in Legal Proceedings:

(a) **At the Time of Charging:** If a defendant does not disclose a fact during questioning or upon being charged that they would logically be expected to mention, this could lead to an adverse inference. Opting to remain silent based on legal counsel does not automatically protect against such an inference. This is particularly relevant if the defendant later presents this fact in their defence during the trial.

(b) **During Trial Proceedings**: Not providing testimony at the trial might result in an adverse inference against the defendant. This is not true if the defendant is physically or mentally unfit to testify.

(c) **Concerning Objects, Substances, or Marks:** Suppose the defendant, at the time of arrest, cannot explain possession of particular objects, substances, or marks found on them. In that case, the court might infer that the defendant withholds information.

(d) **Regarding the Crime Scene:** If the defendant cannot explain their presence at the location of an alleged crime, the court may interpret this as an indication of guilt.

4. The Complexities of Hearsay Evidence

Hearsay evidence encompasses any testimony or documentary evidence introduced in court based on the statements of individuals not present to speak for themselves.

Often perceived as 'secondhand' information, hearsay is traditionally considered less trustworthy than direct evidence due to the inability to validate its accuracy through cross-examination. The formal definition frames hearsay as any assertion not made during live testimony in court but presented to affirm the truth of its content.

This definition extends beyond witnesses relaying information told to them by others; it also encompasses:

(a) **Read Aloud Witness Statements:** Instances where the statements of absent witnesses are read aloud in court instead of the witnesses appearing to testify in person.

(b) **Business Records:** Documentation such as corporate financial records introduced in court as factual evidence.

The primary concern with gossip is its challenge to the defence's ability to scrutinise the veracity of the evidence, a cornerstone of the adversarial legal process. Despite its inherent limitations, hearsay can still be admitted under certain conditions and with appropriate safeguards to ensure the rights of the accused are not compromised.

Taylor is on trial for embezzlement. The primary evidence against them includes a series of emails and financial documents allegedly showing the misappropriation of funds.

During the trial, the prosecution introduces financial statements and emails as evidence. These documents contain information provided by individuals who are not present in court. For instance, an email from an absent co-worker implies Taylor's involvement in the fraudulent activities.

Taylor's defence attorney objects to the emails being admitted as evidence. They argue that since the co-worker who authored the emails is not available for cross-examination, the integrity of the content cannot be adequately assessed, which is a hallmark of hearsay complications.

Additionally, the prosecution presents company account records as evidence of the embezzlement. These records are deemed business documents, which can be an exception to the hearsay rule if they are deemed regular practice for a business to maintain and are used to establish the company's financial activities.

The judge must decide whether the emails and business records can be admitted as evidence. The judge considers the hearsay nature of the emails, the reliability of the business documents, and whether there are sufficient grounds under the rules of evidence to allow for their admission.

The judge rules that the business records can be admitted due to their status as regular business documents. However, the emails will be excluded as hearsay because the defence cannot challenge the co-worker's assertions through cross-examination.

This scenario illustrates the nuanced application of hearsay rules in court proceedings and the importance of the ability to test evidence through cross-examination, underscoring the careful balance courts must maintain between admitting probative evidence and ensuring a fair trial.

5. Criteria for Hearsay Evidence Acceptance

The admissibility of hearsay evidence in legal proceedings is tightly regulated, with specific conditions under which it can be presented in court.

These conditions are designed to maintain the integrity of the judicial process while accommodating instances where hearsay evidence may be sufficiently reliable.

The four distinct categories under which hearsay evidence may be deemed permissible are:

(a) **Statutory Provisions:** Hearsay is permissible if it conforms to exceptions laid out in statutory law. Legislations provide a framework for when hearsay can be introduced, ensuring a clear legal basis for its admission.

(b) **Established Legal Principles:** Certain types of hearsay are admissible based on longstanding legal principles or precedents. This includes evidence that the law has historically been accepted due to its inherent reliability or necessity.

(c) **Consensual Admission:** If all parties involved in the legal proceedings agree to the admission of hearsay evidence, it can be included. This mutual consent acknowledges the value or relevance of the evidence regardless of its hearsay nature.

(d) **Justice Considerations:** In some cases, hearsay may be admitted if it is considered in the interest of justice to do so. This broad category allows the court discretion to admit hearsay evidence when excluding it would undermine the fairness or completeness of the trial.

These categories ensure that hearsay evidence is only admitted under conditions that preserve the fairness of the trial and the rights of the defence while recognising situations where such evidence is necessary for careful consideration of the case.

5.1 Statutory Exceptions to the Hearsay Rule

Within the legal framework, specific statutory exceptions permit the introduction of hearsay evidence. These exceptions are outlined to ensure that the evidence considered in court encompasses all relevant information, even when a witness cannot provide it directly.

The circumstances under which hearsay evidence is statutorily admissible include:

(a) **Unavailability of the Witness:** The testimony of a witness who cannot attend court due to reasons such as death, serious illness, absence from the country with impracticality for attendance, being untraceable despite diligent efforts, or being exempted from testifying due to fear, as authorised by the court, can be presented in the form of written or recorded statements.

(b) **Business Records:** Documents generated or received in a regular business context can be presented as evidence if they meet specific criteria: the document was part of routine business activities, the information provider is believed to have direct knowledge, and the information was transmitted between parties, it was within a business setting.

(c) **Prepared Statements for Criminal Proceedings:** If a person made a statement intending to be used in criminal proceedings and cannot recall the details during the trial, the statement can be introduced as evidence.

(d) **Consistency or Contradictions in Witness Statements:** If a witness's previous statements are consistent with their trial testimony, or if there are discrepancies, these earlier statements may be introduced to either bolster or challenge the witness's credibility.

(e) **Expert Testimony:** Statements made by experts in their field, typically based on specialised knowledge rather than personal observation, can be introduced as evidence.

(f) **Confessions:** Admissions of guilt or statements of confession by a defendant are typically admissible, even if they fall under the hearsay category, given their direct relevance to the case.

These statutory exceptions to the hearsay rule accommodate situations where direct testimony is not possible, ensuring that the court can consider all pertinent information that is relevant and necessary for justice to be served effectively.

5.2 Hearsay Exceptions Based on Legal Principles

Within the legal domain, established principles allow for the admission of hearsay evidence under certain conditions.

These exceptions to the hearsay rule are based on long-standing legal doctrines, aiming to ensure that the evidence presented is both relevant and reliable.

The categories of hearsay that can be admitted by rule of law include:

(a) **Defendant's Statements:** This includes confessions or mixed statements made by the defendant that contain both incriminating and exculpatory elements. These statements are generally admissible due to their direct relevance to the case and the defendant's ownership of the words.

(b) **Contemporaneous Remarks:** Statements made simultaneously with the commission of the offence are considered inherently reliable, as they are unlikely to be premeditated or fabricated. For example, during the commission of an assault, a statement by a bystander, like "Break his neck as we agreed", can be submitted as evidence of premeditation or intent.

(c) **Res Gestae Declarations:** This legal doctrine encompasses statements so closely associated with the event in question that their immediacy and spontaneity imply reliability. They include:

- Overwhelming Emotional Statements: Declarations made while a person is still under the emotional shock of an event suggest their responses are spontaneous and genuine.

- Statements Integral to an Act: Remarks accompanying and elucidating the context of a relevant act, providing insight into its purpose or significance.

- Physical or Mental Condition Exclamations: Utterances concerning a person's physical pain or mental state at the time of an event, which can shed light on the circumstances of the incident.

These rules of law are designed to permit the inclusion of hearsay evidence that, due to its nature and context, carries a high degree of credibility and is vital for the court's understanding of the events in question. By applying these principles, courts can admit hearsay evidence that would otherwise be excluded while preserving the integrity of the judicial process.

Consensual Admission of Hearsay:

The judicial process permits the inclusion of hearsay evidence if all parties involved in the case mutually consent to its admission. This agreement indicates a joint acknowledgement of the evidence's relevance and reliability, allowing it to be considered by the court.

5.3 Judicial Discretion in Evidence Admission

Beyond statutory and common law exceptions, the court possesses a discretionary power to admit hearsay evidence when it aligns with the interests of justice. This provision acts as a judicial safeguard to ensure that the adjudication process is unrestricted by the rules of evidence.

Factors the court must evaluate to exercise this discretion include:

(a) **Probative Importance:** The court assesses the relevance and significance of the statement to the matters being disputed in the case.

(b) **Availability of Other Evidence:** The court considers whether alternative evidence could be presented and the impact of its inclusion or exclusion.

(c) **Overall Case Relevance:** The weight of the evidence in the context of the entire case is appraised, determining how crucial it is to resolve the dispute.

(d) **Context of Statement:** The circumstances under which the statement was made are scrutinised for indications of reliability or potential bias.

(e) **Credibility of the Statement's Source:** The court evaluates the trustworthiness of the person who made the statement.

(f) **Evidence Trustworthiness:** The reliability of the evidence about the statement's creation is examined.

(g) **Possibility of Oral Testimony:** Whether the person who made the statement can testify in court is considered, as direct oral testimony is generally preferred.

(h) **Challenge Difficulty:** The court considers how easily the statement can be contested or verified.

(i) **Potential for Prejudice:** The court assesses the potential for prejudice against either party by admitting the hearsay evidence.

This discretionary power ensures that the court can consider crucial evidence that might otherwise be excluded, thus preserving the flexibility necessary for a fair and just legal process.

5.4 Rules for Admitting Multiple Hearsay

Multiple hearsays, where information is passed through several intermediaries before being presented in court, are subject to stringent admissibility criteria due to the increased risk of distortion or error. The reliability of such evidence diminishes with each relay, hence the need for careful legal control.

To be admitted into court proceedings, multiple hearsay must fall into one of the following categories:

(a) **Business Records:** Documentation generated in the regular course of business is deemed reliable, even if it contains multiple layers of hearsay, due to the standard practices of record-keeping and the presumption of accuracy in business dealings.

(b) **Inconsistent Statements:** If the hearsay includes statements at odds with what has been previously said, they may be introduced to challenge the credibility of a witness or to illustrate a change in the narrative.

(c) **Consistent Statements:** Conversely, hearsay that includes statements aligning with a witness's prior testimony can be admitted to reinforce their reliability or to respond to allegations of fabrication.

(d) **Agreement Among Parties:** Similar to single hearsay, if all parties involved in the trial consent to the admission of multiple hearsay evidence, it may be introduced as part of the proceedings.

(e) **Interest of Justice:** As a catch-all provision, multiple hearsay can also be admitted if the court determines that its probative value significantly outweighs the potential drawbacks and admits it serves the interests of justice. This may apply when the evidence is particularly crucial to the case, and there is sufficient reason to trust its veracity.

These conditions ensure that while the courts recognise the potential value of multiple hearsay, its admission is carefully weighed against the need for accuracy and reliability in the evidence presented before the jury or judge.

6. Understanding Confessions in the Legal Context

In legal proceedings, the concept of a 'confession' encompasses any declaration made by an individual that is, in whole or in part, self-incriminating. This broad definition ensures that any statement that could potentially disadvantage the speaker—regardless of its context or recipient—is scrutinised for its relevance and impact on the case.

Critical aspects of confessions include:

(a) **Wide Scope:** Confessions are not limited to admissions of guilt made directly to authorities or during formal interrogations. Any statement a defendant makes, which could be interpreted as acknowledging responsibility for a crime, falls under this category.

(b) **Verbal and Non-Verbal Admissions:** Confession covers spoken or written admissions and actions or gestures that imply culpability. This recognition of non-verbal communication as potentially self-incriminating evidence underscores the comprehensive approach to evaluating defendants' statements.

(c) **Mixed Statements:** Statements that contain both elements of self-exoneration and self-incrimination are classified as confessions. Exculpatory content does not negate the statement's overall self-incriminating nature, making even complex declarations subject to examination as potential confessions.

This inclusive definition of confessions reflects the legal system's effort to consider all forms of self-incriminating evidence, ensuring that any admission, regardless of its format or the circumstances under which it was made, is appropriately considered in the adjudication process.

Alex is detained by the police on suspicion of involvement in a series of burglaries. During the interrogation, Alex makes several statements to the officers.

Confession: "I was at the scene of the last break-in, but I was just looking out for my friend. I didn't steal anything myself."

(a) **Self-Incriminating Element:** Alex's admission of being present at the crime scene directly links them to the illegal activity, serving as a partial acknowledgment of involvement in the burglary.

(b)   **Exculpatory Element:** At the same time, Alex attempts to distance themselves from the actual act of theft, claiming they did not participate directly in stealing.

Under the legal definition, Alex's statement is considered a confession because it contains elements that are adverse to their own interest, specifically the admission of being at the scene of the crime. The fact that Alex also includes information meant to exonerate themselves (claiming no direct involvement in the theft) does not detract from the statement's classification as a confession. Instead, it exemplifies the nature of mixed statements, which blend self-incriminating admissions with attempts at self-exoneration.

In court, Alex's statement can be introduced as a confession, with the prosecution likely emphasising the admission of presence at the burglary scene. Meanwhile, the defence may focus on the claim of non-involvement in the theft to mitigate Alex's culpability.

This scenario demonstrates how statements made by individuals involved in criminal investigations can be considered confessions, even when they try to present themselves in a partially positive light. It underscores the complexity of evaluating such statements within the legal process and the importance of understanding the full scope of what constitutes a confession.

6.1 Criteria for the Admissibility of Confessions

In the judicial system, confessions are significant pieces of evidence that can decisively impact the outcome of a trial.

Their admissibility is subject to rigorous evaluation to ensure the integrity of the **trial process:**

A confession is considered admissible when it significantly relates to a critical fact under examination in the trial. Its relevance is determined by its capacity to affirm or negate a material aspect of the case, aligning with the principles of evidence.

The defence is entitled to challenge the inclusion of a confession on **specific grounds:**

(a)   **Contesting on the Basis of Falsity:**

•   **Oppression and Misleading Circumstances:** A confession obtained through coercive methods or under conditions that might compromise its truthfulness falls under scrutiny. The defense must establish a clear link between such conditions and the confession to argue for its exclusion.

- **Autonomy of the Confession:** Demonstrating that the confession was made independently of any undue influence or misleading situation validates its admissibility.

(b) **Evidentiary Burden:** When a confession's admissibility is questioned, it becomes the prosecution's responsibility to convincingly demonstrate that the confession was neither coerced through oppressive means nor made under conditions that could question its reliability. Inability to prove this beyond a reasonable doubt necessitates the exclusion of the confession from the trial.

By mandating strict adherence to these criteria, the legal framework ensures that only confessions obtained fairly and relevantly contribute to the judicial decision-making process. This approach underscores the commitment to justice, safeguarding against the misuse of confessions and preserving the fairness of legal proceedings.

The Case of Ella:

Ella is charged with embezzlement based on a confession she made during a police interview. Her defence argues the confession was obtained after hours of questioning without breaks, constituting oppression.

Ella's defence team argues that the oppressive nature of the interrogation—characterised by prolonged questioning without adequate rest—casts doubt on the reliability of her confession.

The prosecution is tasked with demonstrating beyond a reasonable doubt that Ella's confession was made voluntarily and not influenced by the alleged oppressive conditions. The court finds the prosecution unable to satisfactorily prove the confession's voluntariness.

Given the failure to disprove the defence's claims of coercion, Ella's confession is ruled inadmissible. The prosecution must rely on other evidence to pursue the case.

The Case of Marcus:

Marcus faces charges for a robbery. He initially admits to his involvement in a statement to the police but claims during the trial that his confession was made because the officers falsely promised leniency.

Marcus's defence claims the confession was influenced by promises of a lighter sentence, which could render the confession unreliable.

The court examines whether Marcus's confession was truly independent of the alleged promises made by the police.

It falls to the prosecution to prove that Marcus's confession was unaffected by any misleading promises and that it was given freely and knowingly.

The judge determines that the prosecution has not convincingly demonstrated that Marcus's confession was independent of the misleading circumstances. As a result, the confession is excluded from evidence.

These scenarios highlight the judicial processes involved in assessing the admissibility of confessions, emphasising the importance of ensuring that such evidence is obtained fairly and presented with consideration for the defendant's rights and the integrity of the legal system.

6.2 Determining the Admissibility of Confessions

The procedure for assessing the admissibility of confessions varies between the Crown Court and the Magistrates' Court, reflecting their distinct roles in matters of law and fact.

Here's how each court handles the determination:

In the Crown Court:

(a) **Judge's Responsibility:** The judge alone decides on the admissibility of a confession, separating this legal judgment from the jury's evaluation of facts. This decision-making process occurs during a special hearing known as a voir dire, conducted outside the jury's presence.

(b) **Voir Dire Process:** During the voir dire, arguments are presented, and evidence is examined in the absence of the jury to avoid prejudicing their deliberations.

In the Magistrates' Court:

(a) **Joint Fact and Law Determination:** The bench, comprising either a District Judge or lay magistrates, is responsible for resolving both factual disputes and legal questions. This integrated approach means the magistrates must consider the lawfulness of evidence, including confessions, within the broader scope of adjudicating the case.

(b) **Handling Inadmissible Confessions:** If a confession is deemed inadmissible, the magistrates are tasked with disregarding this piece of evidence entirely, proceeding with their deliberations as though the confession was never presented. This requires the magistrates to consciously exclude the inadmissible evidence from their consideration to ensure a fair verdict based solely on permissible evidence.

These procedures underscore the judiciary's commitment to fairness and the principle that all evidence considered in convicting a defendant must be both relevant and legally obtained. By segregating the evaluation of confessions from the jury's purview in the Crown Court and mandating magistrates to disregard inadmissible confessions, the legal system safeguards the integrity of the trial process and the rights of the accused.

7. Judicial Discretion in excluding Evidence to Preserve Fairness

Under the provisions of section 78 of the Police and Criminal Evidence Act 1984 (PACE), courts possess the discretionary power to exclude evidence presented by the prosecution if its inclusion would compromise the fairness of the trial.

This discretionary exclusion is distinct from the mandatory exclusion criteria based on evidence obtained through mistake, untruth, oppressive means, or unreliability due to specific actions.

Here's **how discretionary exclusion operates:**

(a) **Assessment of Fairness:** The court evaluates the impact of admitting the evidence on the overall fairness of the proceedings. This evaluation is comprehensive, considering the circumstances surrounding how the evidence was obtained and its relevance to the case.

(b) **Mandatory vs. Discretionary Exclusion:** While evidence must be excluded if obtained through mistake, untruth, oppression, or specific actions that render it unreliable, the exclusion based on fairness is at the court's discretion. The court may choose to exclude evidence if admitting it would result in an unjust trial, but it is not obligated to do so unless the fairness of the proceedings is significantly jeopardised.

(c) **Circumstances Leading to Discretionary Exclusion:**

- Illegal Searches: Evidence obtained through searches conducted without proper legal authorisation or beyond the scope of granted permissions.

- Identification Evidence Issues: Problems with how identification procedures were conducted, potentially leading to unreliable identification of the defendant.

- Confession Concerns: Issues related to how confessions were obtained, including potential coercion or misleading the defendant.

- Covert Surveillance: The use of surveillance methods that infringe on privacy rights or were conducted without appropriate authorisation.

- Undercover Operations: Operations that might have involved entrapment or other questionable tactics that could prejudice the defendant's case.

(d) **Significance of Breaches:** Typically, a court will invoke its discretion to exclude evidence if the procedural breaches by law enforcement were substantial and significantly impacted the reliability of the evidence or the defendant's rights.

This discretionary power underscores the judiciary's role in ensuring that the integrity of the legal process is maintained and that trials are conducted fairly, with a focus on both the manner in which evidence is obtained and its impact on the justice delivered.

8. Navigating Character Evidence in Legal Proceedings

Character evidence, which can significantly influence the outcome of a trial, is categorised into two distinct types based on the nature of the behaviour it reflects.

This evidence plays a crucial role in shaping the court's perception of the defendant's tendencies and moral fiber:

(a) **Bad Character Evidence:** This includes any information that suggests a propensity towards unlawful or morally questionable behaviour. It encompasses prior convictions, demonstrated patterns of misconduct, or any other actions that may depict the defendant in a negative light. The purpose of introducing bad character evidence is often to establish a pattern of behaviour that supports the prosecution's narrative of the defendant's likelihood of committing the offence in question.

(b) **Good Character Evidence:** In contrast, good character evidence highlights the defendant's virtuous qualities, lack of prior offences, or general conduct that aligns with societal norms and expectations. This type of evidence is typically presented to bolster the defendant's credibility, suggesting that their character makes them less likely to engage in the alleged criminal activity.

The admissibility and impact of character evidence are carefully regulated to prevent undue prejudice that could sway the trial's fairness. For bad character evidence to be introduced, it must meet specific legal criteria and be deemed relevant to the case at hand, such as demonstrating motive, opportunity, or a pattern of similar behaviour. Similarly, good character evidence is weighed for its ability to support the defendant's claims of innocence or mitigate the severity of their actions.

In navigating character evidence, courts must balance the need to present a comprehensive view of the defendant's behaviour with the imperative to conduct a fair and impartial trial, ensuring that the evidence's probative value is not overshadowed by its potential to prejudice the jury or judge.

8.1 Guidelines for the Use of Bad Character Evidence

The legal framework outlines seven specific conditions under which evidence of a defendant's bad character may be introduced in court, ensuring its application is both pertinent and just.

These criteria serve to guide the admissibility of such evidence, reflecting a careful balance between the necessity of this evidence for the case and the protection of the defendant's rights:

(a) **Consensus Among Parties:** When all parties involved in the trial consent, bad character evidence can be admitted. This consensus recognises the relevance and potential impact of the evidence on the proceedings.

(b) **Initiated by the Defendant:** Includes situations where the defendant voluntarily presents bad character evidence about themselves or addresses it when questioned during cross-examination.

(c) **Necessity for Contextual Understanding:** If bad character evidence is crucial for comprehending other evidence within the case, contributing significantly to the overall narrative, it is deemed admissible.

(d) **Significance to Crucial Issues:** Evidence that sheds light on vital aspects of the case, such as the defendant's inclination towards similar unlawful actions or dishonesty, can be introduced. This is particularly relevant for showing patterns of conduct similar to the alleged crime.

(e) **Inter-defendant Discrepancies:** Evidence of bad character that is highly probative regarding disputes between the defendant and co-defendant(s) may be permitted.

(f) **Counteracting Misleading Impressions:** Evidence that rectifies any misleading portrayal by the defendant regarding their character, whether made during trial or in pre-trial statements, is admissible.

(g) **Rebuttal of Character Attacks:** If the defendant or their counsel impugns someone else's character or insinuates such through questioning, evidence of the defendant's own bad character becomes relevant and admissible.

These guidelines delineate the circumstances under which bad character evidence may enter the courtroom, ensuring that its inclusion serves the interests of justice without unduly prejudicing the defendant's right to a fair trial.

Admitting Bad Character Evidence for Explanatory Purposes:

The admissibility of bad character evidence as important explanatory evidence is a critical aspect of ensuring the jury has a comprehensive understanding of the case.

Such evidence is considered permissible under specific conditions:

(a) **Necessity for Understanding:** If omitting the bad character evidence would leave the jury unable to fully grasp the significance or context of other evidence presented in the trial, its inclusion becomes essential. This criterion acknowledges that certain aspects of a case can only be effectively understood in light of the defendant's previous actions or patterns of behaviour.

(b) **Significant Value:** The evidence must contribute significantly to the jury's overall understanding of the case. Its inclusion should offer substantial insight, clarifying the narrative or elucidating connections between various pieces of evidence.

(c) **Overlap with Propensity Evidence:** There is often a convergence between bad character evidence admitted for its explanatory value and evidence showing a propensity towards certain behaviours. While the primary goal of explanatory evidence is to aid in understanding the case's context, it may also indirectly suggest a likelihood of the defendant acting in a manner consistent with their character.

This gateway ensures that the jury receives a full picture of the case, enabling a more informed deliberation by illuminating the context and relevance of the evidence within the broader narrative of the proceedings.

Admitting Evidence based on Propensity:

The admission of bad character evidence when it pertains to "an important matter in issue between the prosecution and the defence" serves as a pivotal mechanism in legal proceedings.

This gateway allows for the inclusion of evidence indicating a defendant's propensity to engage in similar misconduct or to be untruthful, under specific considerations:

(a) **Definition of Similar Offence:** The concept of similarity extends beyond identical offences to encompass a broader range of activities reflecting parallel behavioural patterns. Thus, offences that share core characteristics with the charged conduct can be considered indicative of propensity, providing a basis for the admission of bad character evidence.

(b) **Establishing Propensity:** While there is no fixed threshold for the number of prior incidents required to demonstrate propensity, the presence of multiple instances strengthens the argument for a behavioural pattern. A singular past offence may suffice if it shares distinctive features with the current charge, highlighting a unique or specific modus operandi.

(c) **Consideration of Conviction History:** The relevance of previous convictions, including those that are old or spent, is assessed in the context of their similarity to the current charge. The distinctiveness and rarity of the behaviours involved play a significant role in determining their probative value as evidence of propensity.

(d) **Untruthfulness as Evidence of Propensity:** Evidence showcasing a tendency towards dishonesty is admissible when deceit is integral to the offence in question. This aspect is narrowly interpreted to ensure that evidence of dishonest behaviour is directly relevant to the matters being contested in the current case, rather than serving as a general character indictment.

This gateway underscores the nuanced approach required in evaluating bad character evidence, ensuring its admission is not only relevant to the specific disputes at hand but also materially significant to the case's outcome. By carefully delineating the parameters for including propensity evidence, the legal system safeguards the fairness of the trial while allowing the jury to consider pertinent aspects of the defendant's character.

Evidence between Co-Defendants: Substantial Probative Value:

The introduction of bad character evidence based on its substantial probative value regarding disputes between co-defendants represents a critical aspect of legal proceedings, especially in cases involving "cut-throat" defences. This scenario occurs when co-defendants accuse each other, attempting to attribute the responsibility for the crime to one another.

Key considerations for this gateway include:

(a) **Application in Co-Defendant Disputes:** When co-defendants present conflicting defences, bad character evidence may be utilised to suggest that one party, given their history of similar misconduct, is more likely to have committed the current offence. This strategy is often employed in "cut-throat" situations where the blame is shifted from one defendant to another.

(b) **Threshold for Admissibility:** The criterion for introducing such evidence is not merely its relevance to the case but its substantial probative value. This denotes that the evidence must significantly contribute to resolving a crucial dispute between the co-defendants, offering clear insight into the likelihood of one party's involvement in the offence.

(c) **Importance of the Matter in Issue:** The evidence must pertain to an essential aspect of the case under contention between the co-defendants. Its admission is predicated on the ability to illuminate significant questions regarding the roles and responsibilities of each party involved in the alleged crime.

This gateway emphasises the necessity of a rigorous evaluation process to determine the admissibility of bad character evidence in situations where co-defendants' narratives conflict. By setting a higher threshold of "substantial probative value," the legal system ensures that only evidence with a significant impact on the resolution of critical issues between co-defendants is considered, thereby upholding the principles of fairness and relevance in the judicial process.

Admissibility Following Defendant's Attack on Another' s Character:

The legal framework allows for the introduction of a defendant's bad character evidence as a countermeasure when the defendant has initiated an attack on another individual's character. This provision ensures a level of accountability and fairness in the presentation of evidence.

The **conditions** under which the defendant's bad character becomes relevant include:

(a) **Scope of the Attack:** The defendant's actions that qualify as an attack on character are broadly defined. These actions can occur at various stages of the legal process, not limited to the trial's evidence phase. Attacks made during questioning under caution, upon being charged, or through statements made by the defence in court are encompassed within this rule.

(b) **Actions by Defence Counsel:** If the defence counsel engages in cross-examination or introduces evidence aiming to discredit a witness, imply bias, highlight past misconduct, or allege police misconduct, this too can trigger the admissibility of the defendant's bad character. The strategic choice to undermine the credibility of others opens the door to scrutiny of the defendant's own character.

(c) **Variety of Allegations:** The range of actions considered an attack on character is extensive. It includes, but is not limited to, insinuations of bias, the revelation of previous convictions, and accusations against law enforcement or any other party involved in the case. Such tactics by the defence are met with the potential introduction of evidence reflecting negatively on the defendant's character.

This gateway underscores the principle that attempts to undermine the character of witnesses, victims, or other parties involved in the case can have reciprocal consequences for the defendant. By allowing the admission of bad character evidence under these circumstances, the legal system maintains a balance, ensuring that both the prosecution and defence adhere to standards of fairness and relevance in their arguments and evidence presentation.

8.2 Steps for Introducing Bad Character Evidence of the Defendant

The process for introducing a defendant's bad character evidence into court proceedings involves specific procedural steps designed to ensure fairness and transparency.

Both the prosecution and defence are required to adhere to **these steps:**

(a) **Notice Requirement:** The prosecution, intending to present bad character evidence, must formally notify the defence and the court. This notification must be made using a prescribed form and served within specific time frames: within 28 days following a not guilty plea in the Magistrates' Court, and within 14 days after a not guilty plea in the Crown Court.

(b) **Response by the Defendant:** If the defendant, or their legal representative, seeks to challenge the admissibility of the bad character evidence, they must respond using a designated form to oppose the notice. This opposition notice outlines the basis for contesting the evidence's inclusion in the trial.

(c) **Decision-making Process:** The admissibility of the bad character evidence is typically determined during a pre-trial hearing. However, it may also be resolved on the trial day itself, outside the jury's presence in the Crown Court, to prevent any potential prejudice. This decision is made by the judge, who evaluates the evidence's relevance and potential impact on the trial's fairness.

This structured approach to admitting bad character evidence ensures that both sides have the opportunity to present their arguments regarding the evidence's relevance and appropriateness. By mandating formal notices and allowing for responses, the legal system upholds the principles of due process and equitable treatment for the defendant while providing the court with crucial information to inform its decisions.

8.3 Judicial Discretion in Excluding Bad Character Evidence of the Defendant

The court holds the authority to exclude a defendant's bad character evidence, even if it fits within one of the seven admissibility gateways, should its inclusion potentially compromise the fairness of the trial.

This power is particularly emphasised under two specific circumstances:

(a) **Important Matters in Issue & Character Attacks:** When evidence is presented under the gateways concerning "an important matter in issue between the prosecution and defence" or instances where "the defendant attacked another's character," the court faces a critical decision. If the defence successfully petitions to exclude this evidence, citing concerns over trial fairness, the court must carefully evaluate the potential for prejudice.

(b) **Exclusion Criteria:** The court is compelled to deny admission of the evidence if it concludes that its presence would unjustly affect the proceedings. This decision-making process includes considering the temporal distance between the events constituting the bad character evidence and the charged offence, assessing whether the lapse in time diminishes the evidence's relevance or increases the risk of unfairness.

(c) **Contrast with Section 78 PACE 1984:** This specific provision for excluding bad character evidence underlines a more stringent requirement compared to the broader discretion granted by Section 78 of PACE 1984. While Section 78 allows the court the option to refuse evidence that might adversely impact trial fairness, the rules for excluding evidence under the highlighted gateways mandate non-admission if it's determined that such evidence would indeed result in an unfair trial.

This framework underscores the legal system's commitment to maintaining the integrity of the judicial process, ensuring that the inclusion of bad character evidence does not undermine the fundamental principle of a fair trial. The court's obligation to reject evidence under these conditions reflects a protective measure designed to guard against the potential for prejudice, affirming the priority of justice in the proceedings.

8.4 Presentation of Good Character Evidence

Good character evidence is crucial in illustrating an individual's tendency away from engaging in misconduct, committing offences, or exhibiting other undesirable behaviour. Demonstrated through an absence of criminal history or notable positive actions such as significant voluntary efforts or public service, this evidence underscores the defendant's integrity.

Good Character Direction:

Defendants lacking prior convictions are granted a judicial instruction known as a Good Character Direction to the jury.

This direction is bifurcated into:

(a)   **Propensity Aspect:** Indicates that an individual of good character is less likely to be responsible for the offence in question.

(b) **Credibility Aspect:** Asserts that an individual of reputable character should be considered more trustworthy in their proclamations of innocence, whether stated before or during the trial.

Eligibility for Good Character Direction:

(a) **Past Convictions:** Defendants with historical, minor convictions unrelated to the current charge are viewed as possessing compelling good character, qualifying them for both propensity and credibility aspects of the Good Character Direction.

(b) **Presence of Other Bad Character Evidence:** If the prosecution introduces additional bad character evidence, the feasibility of issuing a Good Character Direction is reduced.

(c) **Discretionary Considerations:** In instances where the defendant has a clear record, and the prosecution chooses not to rely on available bad character evidence, the issuance of a Good Character Direction lies within the judge's discretion.

Employing the Good Character Direction ensures the jury considers the defendant's moral standing and history of lawful behaviour, providing a comprehensive view of their character about the charges faced.

CHAPTER 8. LEGAL PROCEDURES DURING TRIAL IN MAGISTRATES' AND CROWN COURTS

1. Responsibility and Level of Proof

In legal trials, the obligation to demonstrate the defendant's guilt rests with the prosecution. This involves convincing either the Magistrates' Court bench Di, a strict judge, or the jury in the Crown Court that the defendant committed the offence beyond any reasonable doubt. The prosecution initiates the presentation of evidence by summoning witnesses, ranging from the victim and eyewitnesses to police officers and specialists.

Following the prosecution, the defence can present its case, potentially including testimony from the defendant. Should the defendant decide to testify, their evidence is heard before any other witnesses for the defence, establishing the sequence and structure of the trial process.

2. Overview of the typical criminal stages

(a) **Prosecution Opening Speech:** The trial begins with the prosecution's opening statement, where the prosecutor outlines the allegations against the defendant and sets out the critical evidence that will be presented.

(b) **Prosecution Calls Witnesses:** The prosecution presents its case by calling witnesses, including the victim, law enforcement officials, and any other eyewitnesses or experts relevant to the case.

(c) **Defence Application of No Case to Answer [if applicable]:** After the prosecution has presented its evidence, the defence may argue that there is insufficient evidence for the case to continue. If the court agrees, the case is dismissed.

(d) **Defence Calls Witnesses:** If the trial continues, the defence can present its case by calling its witnesses, including potentially the defendant.

(e) **Jury Deliberation [Crown Court only]:** In cases tried by a jury, once all evidence has been presented and both sides have made their closing arguments, the jury retires to deliberate and reach a verdict.

(f) **Judge Summing Up [Crown Court only]:** Before the jury deliberates, the judge summarises the evidence and clarifies any legal principles the jury must consider to reach their verdict.

(g) **Verdict:** The bench or judge (in the Magistrates' Court) or the jury (in the Crown Court) delivers the verdict, stating whether the defendant is guilty.

(h) **Pre-Sentence Reports [if applicable]:** If the defendant is found guilty, the court may order pre-sentence reports to gather more information about the defendant to aid in sentencing.

(i) **Sentencing:** Finally, depending on the trial's findings and any pre-sentence reports, the bench (Magistrates' Court) or judge (Crown Court) passes the sentence, imposing the appropriate punishment on the defendant.

3. Initial Questioning of Witnesses

During a trial, each witness undergoes an initial round of questioning by the party that summoned them to testify. For instance, a witness for the prosecution will first be questioned by the prosecution team in what's known as the examination in chief.

Subsequently, the opposing legal team will question the same witness, termed a cross-examination. The examination in chief is characterised by using open-ended questions that do not hint at a particular response. Such questions typically begin with interrogatives like who, what, where, when, why, or how and are designed to elicit expansive, informative responses.

They can also be framed as requests for the witness to narrate or elaborate on their previous statements.

For example, the lawyer might say, "Please describe what you witnessed on the morning of the incident."

4. The Process of Cross-Examination

Following the conclusion of the examination in chief, the witness enters the cross-examination phase conducted by the opposing legal party.

The primary objective of the cross-examiner is to scrutinise the testimony provided during the examination in chief and introduce their client's perspective to the evidence presented. Unlike in the examination in chief, during cross-examination, the questioning attorney is permitted to pose leading questions.

These are inquiries constructed to imply or contain the answer within the question itself. Such questions are strategically employed to challenge the witness's earlier statements and to reaffirm the cross-examiner's narrative of the events.

An example of a leading question in cross-examination might be:

"Isn't it true that you were at the shopping centre at 9 p.m. on the night of the incident, not at home as you claimed during the examination in chief?"

This question suggests the answer (that the witness was at the shopping centre) and is designed to challenge the witness's previous testimony of being at home at the specified time.

5. Eligibility and Obligation to Testify in Court

The terms "competence" and "comparability" deal with a witness's eligibility and requirement to testify in court. Competence refers to the capability of a witness to understand and respond to questions in a manner that the court can comprehend. Witnesses are deemed competent if they can grasp the questions or communicate intelligible answers.

Except for the defendant and their spouse or civil partner, all witnesses are typically eligible to testify for the side that has summoned them. They can be mandated to do so if they are competent.

5.1 Position of the Defendant

During their trial, the defendant is not obligated to testify for the prosecution and is not forced to testify for their defence.

However, there may be implications if the defendant chooses to remain silent:

(a) **Right to Silence:** The defendant has a legal right not to testify.

(b) **Inferences Drawn by the Jury:** The jury may infer appropriate conclusions from the defendant's silence.

(c) **No Assumption of Guilt:** The defendant's choice not to testify cannot be the sole evidence of their guilt, but it can be considered, depending on the case specifics.

(d) **Assessment of Silence:** The jury might interpret the defendant's silence as an indication that they have no defence against the charges, mainly if it appears that they are avoiding cross-examination.

Ultimately, the jury must decide if it's reasonable to interpret the defendant's silence negatively. A conviction cannot be based solely on an adverse inference drawn from the defendant's decision not to testify.

John Doe is on trial for alleged fraud. The prosecution presents a series of witnesses who testify about John's involvement in the scheme. After the prosecution rests its case, it's the defence's turn.

The defence has a witness, Mrs Smith, who is elderly and somewhat hard of hearing. The court must determine if she is competent to testify, meaning she must understand the questions and provide answers that the court can understand. If Mrs. Smith meets these criteria, she is deemed competent.

Mrs Smith, once deemed competent, is also compellable by the defence, which means she can be legally required to testify if necessary.

John Doe must decide whether to testify in his defence. As the defendant, he is competent to testify for the defence but not compellable; he cannot be forced to take the stand.

If John chooses not to testify, the jury will receive instructions similar to the specimen direction outlined above. They will be told to consider his silence in their deliberations and that they cannot convict him solely because he chose not to testify.

The jury will deliberate, considering John's right to remain silent against the prosecution's evidence. They must decide if his silence is due to a lack of a credible defence or simply an exercise of his legal rights.

In the end, John's decision not to testify is just one of many factors the jury will consider in reaching their verdict. They must weigh this decision against the evidence presented during the trial.

5.2 Testifying Spouses or Civil Partners

When it comes to the testimony of a defendant's spouse or civil partner, the legal framework provides specific guidelines:

(a) **General Rule:** Generally, for the prosecution or a co-defendant, the defendant's spouse or civil partner can testify if they wish but cannot be legally compelled to do so.

(b) **Exceptions:** In cases where the offence is personal, such as an assault or threat against them or a minor, or in cases involving sexual offences against a child, the spouse or civil partner is both competent and can be required to testify. This also extends to charges of attempting, conspiring, aiding, or abetting these crimes.

(c) **Defendant's Right:** For the defence, the spouse or civil partner can give evidence and be required to do so, provided they are not jointly charged with the offence.

5.3 Co-Defendants as Witnesses

The rules regarding co-defendants' eligibility to testify are as follows:

(a) **For Prosecution:** Co-defendants are neither eligible to testify nor can they be forced to testify for the prosecution.

(b) **For Defence:** Co-defendants can testify for the defence if they choose, but they cannot be compelled to do so.

(c) **Change in Status:** If a co-defendant admits guilt by pleading or if the charges against them are dismissed, their status shifts. They then become an ordinary witness, meaning they can testify and be compelled to do so by either the prosecution or the defence.

6. Provisions for Vulnerable Witnesses

The court can implement special measures to support vulnerable witnesses during their testimony.

These measures are aimed at individuals who may find the court environment intimidating or distressing, including:

(a) **Youthful Witnesses:** Individuals who are below the age of 18 years.

(b) **Witnesses with Disabilities or Disorders:** Those who can give evidence might be impaired due to physical, mental, or psychological conditions.

(c) **Witnesses Intimidated by the Court Setting:** Individuals whose capacity to testify is affected by fear or anxiety related to the court proceedings.

(d) **Victims of Sexual Crimes:** Complainants in cases involving sexual offences often require additional protection and privacy.

(e) **Witnesses of Certain Violent Crimes:** Specifically, those who have witnessed gun or knife-related offences.

Special Measures Available:

(a) **Visual Barriers:** Using screens can prevent witnesses from facing the defendant directly, alleviating stress or fear.

(b) **Remote Testimony:** Allowing witnesses to give evidence through a video link facilitates participation from a secure location.

(c) **Relaxed Court Formalities:** Court officials may remove traditional attire, such as wigs and gowns, to create a less formal atmosphere.

(d) **Private Testimony:** Conducting the witness's testimony in private, away from the public and press, to ensure confidentiality and reduce pressure.

(e) **Pre-recorded Evidence:** Witnesses may record their evidence, which is presented during the trial, in advance.

(f) **Intermediary Assistance:** Using a trained professional to facilitate communication between the witness and the court, ensuring the witness's evidence is conveyed.

Furthermore, the court may decide that any witness, except the defendant, can testify via video link to promote the effective administration of justice. These special measures are part of a broader effort to make the judicial process more accessible and less daunting for those who might otherwise struggle to participate fully and truthfully.

7. Challenging the Sufficiency of Prosecution Evidence

Following the prosecution's presentation of its case, the defence can argue that there is no case to answer.

This means contending that the evidence presented by the prosecution is insufficient to establish a prima facie case against the defendant. The grounds for this submission include the prosecution's failure to provide evidence on one or more essential elements of the offence or if the evidence presented is so unreliable that no reasonable judge, jury, or bench could base a conviction on it.

In the Crown Court, this argument is made in the absence of the jury and is evaluated by the judge. A successful submission results in the defendant's immediate acquittal, while a rejection leads to the continuation of the trial, with the defence then presenting its case, possibly including testimony from witnesses.

8. Protocols for Addressing Court Officials

How court officials are addressed varies between the Magistrates' Court and the Crown Court, reflecting traditional protocols and the level of formality associated with each court setting.

In the Magistrates' Court, individual magistrates are addressed directly as "Sir" or "Madam," and collectively, they are referred to as "Your Worships." A District Judge within the same court is also addressed as "Sir" or "Madam." In contrast, in the Crown Court, the judge is addressed as "Your Honour" during direct address or referred to as "His or Her Honour Judge [Surname]" in third-person narratives. These modes of address maintain the decorum and respect integral to the judicial process.

9. Solicitor's Ethical Obligations in Court Proceedings

The Solicitor's Code of Conduct provides a framework of outcomes and corresponding behaviours that illustrate solicitors' ethical responsibilities towards the court.

These responsibilities ensure the integrity of legal proceedings and are integral to maintaining public trust in the legal system.

Critical aspects of these duties include:

(a) **Honesty in Court:** Solicitors must not knowingly or recklessly mislead the court through direct actions or by aiding others in deception.

(b) **Obedience to Court Orders:** Solicitors must comply with all court orders and advise their clients to do the same.

(c) **Preventing Contempt:** Solicitors should avoid actions that would place themselves in contempt of court and inform the court if an inadvertent error has led to misinformation.

(d) **Prioritisation of Court Duties:** When a solicitor's duties to the court conflict with client obligations, the duty to the court must take precedence.

(e) **Non-interference with Witnesses:** Solicitors must refrain from improperly influencing witnesses or tampering with evidence.

(f) **Discretion in Court Appearances:** A solicitor should not appear for a client if it is anticipated that they, or someone from their firm, may be called as a witness to avoid conflicts of interest.

(g) **Sensitive Handling of Issues:** Ensuring that sensitive issues, particularly those involving child witnesses, are handled with the utmost care to prevent misuse of such situations.

These duties are typically explored in-depth during Professional Conduct lectures, providing solicitors with clear guidelines on acting ethically and responsibly in their professional responsibilities within the legal system.

10. Prevailing Ethical Challenges in Legal Representation

10.1 Client Confesses Guilt but Intends to Plead Not Guilty

When a client privately acknowledges their guilt yet intends to plead not guilty, the solicitor faces a complex ethical situation.

The solicitor must provide candid advice regarding the evidence against the client and the potential benefits of entering a guilty plea. Should the client persist with their decision to plead not guilty, the solicitor may continue to represent them but is ethically barred from presenting false assertions or fabricated defences in court.

Their role is limited to challenging the prosecution's evidence's credibility without advancing a fabricated narrative. If the client desires to present a false account or defence, the solicitor must withdraw from representation to uphold their duty of honesty to the court.

10.2 Client Denies Guilt but Chooses to Plead Guilty

In the reverse scenario, where a client denies guilt but opts for a guilty plea, possibly to evade the ordeal of a trial, the solicitor must ensure the client is fully informed about their available defences.

If the client remains steadfast in their decision to plead guilty, the solicitor's role adjusts to ensure compliance with legal ethics. They may continue to act on the client's behalf but cannot imply innocence during mitigation, as this would contradict the admission of guilt inherent in the guilty plea.

To do so would mislead the court and provoke judicial inquiry into the plea's validity, thus violating the solicitor's professional obligation to maintain courtroom integrity.

10.3 Legal Counsel's Obligation to Clarify Legal Principles

Legal representatives are tasked with clarifying points of law for the court, an obligation that persists even when it may not align with the client's interests. This duty to inform the court accurately extends to ensuring that legal principles are correctly applied.

However, it only necessitates aiding the court with factual discrepancies unless such omissions would result in misleading the court.

Representation in Magistrates' Court:

When the Magistrates' Court setting lacks fully qualified legal professionals—such as when a legal advisor has not yet completed their qualifications or the prosecution's case is presented by a caseworker without formal legal training—the defence solicitor often assumes a pivotal role. It may fall upon the defence solicitor to guide the court on matters such as the admissibility of evidence or nuances in the legal definitions of offences.

In these scenarios, the defence solicitor's comprehensive legal knowledge becomes an essential asset to the court, ensuring that legal proceedings are conducted by established legal standards and principles.

Mr Lee is on trial in the Magistrates' Court for a traffic offence. The prosecution caseworker, who is not a qualified solicitor, presents evidence obtained from a speed camera. The prosecution caseworker is unfamiliar with the latest case law regarding the admissibility of certain types of speed camera evidence.

During the trial, it becomes apparent to Mr Lee's legally qualified defence solicitor that the prosecution relies on evidence that a recent ruling has been deemed inadmissible without proper calibration records. The defence solicitor recognises that the prosecution needs to be made aware of this development in law and that the Magistrates' bench, consisting of laypeople, is likely to be equally uninformed.

Given the solicitor's ethical duty to assist the court on points of law, even if it could potentially disadvantage Mr Lee's defence, the solicitor informs the court about the recent ruling. He clarifies the legal requirements for the admissibility of speed camera evidence, emphasising the need for calibration records.

In this scenario, the defence solicitor fulfils his professional duty to ensure the court is accurately informed about the law, even though this information could lead to the exclusion of crucial evidence from the prosecution's case, which might have otherwise supported Mr Lee's defence. This ethical obligation upholds the integrity of the legal process, ensuring that the court's verdict is based on correctly applied legal standards.

10.4 Managing Dual Representation and Conflicts of Interest

Solicitors must navigate potential conflicts of interest cautiously, mainly when representing multiple clients within the same case.

The **ethical guidelines** stipulate:

(a) **Unified Defence:** A solicitor may represent multiple defendants concurrently, provided that the narratives and interests of these clients do not diverge or conflict. This collective representation is contingent on the compatibility of the defendants' accounts and defence strategies.

(b) **The emergence of Conflicts:** Should a conflict arise after a solicitor has agreed to represent multiple defendants—where their stories diverge or their defences become antagonistic—the solicitor must typically cease representation for all involved parties to avoid a breach of ethical duties.

(c) **Continued Representation:** There is an exception that allows a solicitor to continue representing one client after a conflict has emerged. This is permissible only if the solicitor can ensure that the confidentiality and interests of the other client are fully protected and not jeopardised by the continued representation.

These provisions are designed to prevent any compromise of the solicitor's duty to provide impartial and dedicated representation to each client and to protect confidential information. By adhering to these standards, solicitors maintain the integrity of the legal process and the trust placed in them by their clients.

Solicitor Ms Edwards represents two clients, Mr Brown and Mr Green, who have been charged with conspiracy to commit burglary. Initially, both clients provided Ms Edwards with accounts that suggested a joint defence strategy was viable.

As the case progresses, it becomes clear that Mr Brown wishes to change his account, now implicating Mr Green as the mastermind behind the burglary while claiming he was merely present at the wrong time. This new account directly conflicts with Mr Green's version of events, which maintains that he was not involved and that Mr Brown acted independently.

Upon this revelation, Ms. Edwards faces a conflict of interest. Her professional obligations prevent her from representing both defendants because their defences are no longer aligned and are, in fact, mutually incriminating. To continue representing both would compromise her duty of confidentiality and the obligation to act in the best interest of each client without bias.

In line with her ethical duties, Ms. Edwards withdraws from representing Mr. Brown and Mr. Green. Alternatively, if it were clear that continuing to represent Mr Green would not breach the confidentiality of Mr Brown (perhaps due to Mr Brown's willingness to have his role openly acknowledged in court), Ms Edwards could choose to continue representing Mr Green alone.

This example illustrates the delicate balance solicitors must maintain when representing multiple clients and the imperative to avoid conflicts of interest to uphold the integrity of the legal profession and the fairness of the judicial process.

CHAPTER 9. FRAME-WORK FOR SENTEN-CING

1. Determination of Sentence

Upon a guilty verdict or admission of guilt by the defendant, the court proceeds to the sentencing phase. The court's considerations for sentencing encompass several objectives: to penalise the offender, to contribute to the reduction of crime, to promote the offender's rehabilitation, to protect the public, and to secure restitution from the offender.

To inform its decision on the most suitable sentence, the court may request detailed pre-sentence reports from probation services or mental health assessments.

2. Application of Sentencing Guidelines

Courts utilise established sentencing guidelines to assure uniformity in sentencing for comparable offences. These guidelines provide a reference point for sentencing and enumerate factors that could aggravate or mitigate the severity of the sentence.

While courts are generally required to adhere to these guidelines, deviations are permitted if adherence would result in an unjust outcome in the case's specific circumstances.

3. Assessing the Gravity of an Offence (Considering Aggravating and Mitigating Elements)

The court must weigh various factors that influence the gravity of the offence when determining an appropriate sentence. These factors are to be considered for all relevant offences. Beyond the general guidance on assessing seriousness, specific guidelines tailored to particular offences must be considered during sentencing.

Aggravating Factors that are Mandatory Considerations:

(a) **Past Convictions:** The court must evaluate previous convictions when relevant and reasonable, considering the nature of those past offences and the time elapsed since those convictions.

(b) **Bail Status:** Committing an offence while on bail aggravates the seriousness.

(c) **Hate Crimes:** Offences aggravated by racial or religious hostility or hostility towards the victim's sexual orientation, transgender identity, or disability are taken particularly seriously.

Aggravating Factors that are Discretionary:

(a) **Premeditation**: If the offence was planned.

(b) **Group Involvement:** Offences committed with others.

(c) **Vulnerability of Victim:** Specifically targeting vulnerable individuals.

(d) **Influence of Substances:** Committing an offence under the influence of drugs or alcohol.

(e) **Breach of Trust:** Abusing a position of trust.

(f) **Use of Weapons:** Bringing weapons into play during the offence.

(g) **Malicious Intent:** Gratuitous violence or significant property damage.

(h) **Disregard for Public Services:** Offences affecting those providing a public service.

(i) **Value of Damage:** High monetary or sentimental value of the property involved.

(j) **Non-compliance with Previous Sentences:** Not adhering to the terms of prior sentences.

Mitigating Factors the Court May Consider:

(a) **Spontaneity**: An offence committed impulsively.

(b) **Provocation**: When the defendant was highly provoked.

(c) **Defendant's Circumstances:** Including disability, mental illness, or extreme youth or age.

(d) **Role in Offence:** A minor role in the crime.

(e) **Fear as a Motivator:** Actions taken out of fear.

(f) **Efforts to Address Harm:** Attempts to make reparations with the victim.

These factors give the court a structured approach to sentence determination, ensuring a fair and proportional response to the crime committed.

4. Decision between Concurrent and Consecutive Sentences

When deciding on the sentencing for an offender convicted of multiple offences, the court is guided by the principle of totality.

This principle ensures that the collective sentence accurately reflects the offender's conduct without being excessively severe.

(a) **Concurrent Sentences:** Typically, if the offences are interrelated or stem from the same incident, the sentences for each offence will run concurrently—that is, they will overlap in time. This approach is based on the understanding that the offences are part of a singular episode of wrongdoing.

(b) **Consecutive Sentences:** In contrast, the court may impose consecutive sentences if the offences are separate instances of misconduct. Here, the offender serves the sentence for one offence followed by the sentence for the subsequent offence, and so on, reflecting the distinct nature of each crime.

In applying consecutive sentences, the court must meticulously apply the totality principle to prevent the total time of incarceration from exceeding a level that would be considered just and fair in light of the combined seriousness of the offences.

Mr. Thompson has been found guilty of three separate charges: burglary, driving under the influence (DUI), and assault. The burglary and assault happened during the same incident—a break-in at a home where a confrontation with the homeowner occurred. The DUI charge, however, relates to an event a week before the burglary.

The court decides that the sentences for burglary and assault should run concurrently. Since these offences were part of the same criminal act, serving these sentences simultaneously reflects the interconnectedness of the actions.

Conversely, because the DUI happened independently of the burglary and assault, the court imposes a consecutive sentence for this offence. After Mr. Thompson completes his sentence for the burglary and assault, he will then serve the sentence for the DUI.

By doing so, the court aims to ensure that the total time Mr Thompson spends in custody is proportionate to the seriousness of all the offences combined, adhering to the principle of totality. Mr. Thompson's overall sentence thus reflects both the individual and collective gravity of his actions.

5. Presentation of Mitigating Circumstances

In the sentencing phase of a trial, the court considers various mitigating factors that may lead to a reduced sentence. The defence attorney will highlight these factors to the court through a plea in mitigation.

Reduction for Admission of Guilt:

A defendant who admits to the crime before the trial can expect a lighter sentence in recognition of their early guilty plea. This acknowledgement conserves judicial resources and spares witnesses from the stress of trial proceedings. The sooner the admission of guilt is made, the more significant the sentence reduction, with the maximum reduction being a one-third decrease if the plea is entered at the earliest stage.

Mitigating Factors About the Crime:

Sentencing guidelines provide specific mitigating elements related to the nature of the crime, such as the value involved in property crimes or crimes carried out without premeditation. The defence lawyer will seek to highlight these factors while minimising any aspects of the crime that could be aggravating.

Personal Mitigating Factors:

Consideration is also given to the personal circumstances of the defendant that may have influenced their behaviour, including age, physical or mental health, previously unblemished character, employment status, family responsibilities, positive changes made since the offence, genuine remorse, and steps taken to prevent future offences. These factors can significantly influence the court's discretion in determining the appropriate sentence.

6. Sentencing Options Available to Courts

When imposing a sentence, courts must determine the most appropriate type of punishment considering the nature of the offence and the offender's circumstances.

The sentencing powers of courts vary depending on their level:

(a) **Magistrates' Court Limitations:** This court can sentence an offender to a maximum of six months imprisonment for a single summary offence or a single either-way offence. The Magistrates' Court can impose sentences totalling up to 12 months for multiple either-way offences.

(b) **Crown Court Sentencing:** The Crown Court has the authority to issue sentences up to the statutory maximum for any offence. For example, the maximum custodial sentence for Actual Bodily Harm (ABH) is five years.

These sentencing parameters ensure that the punishment for an offence is proportionate to the crime's gravity and to the powers vested in each court.

6.1 Threshold for Imprisonment

A court may consider a custodial sentence only when the offence is severe enough to surpass the custody threshold. This principle holds that a custodial sentence should not be issued if the offence can be appropriately addressed with a fine or a community penalty. The decision to incarcerate is reserved for cases where the nature and severity of the offence render non-custodial sentences inadequate.

Once the custody threshold is crossed, the court refers to the relevant sentencing guidelines to ascertain the minimum necessary sentence length reflecting the offence's severity. The guiding principle is to impose the shortest sentence proportionate to the offence's seriousness. Generally, an offender is expected to serve half of their sentence in prison, with the remainder served on licence in the community.

During the licence period, adherence to specific conditions is mandated, and any violation or commission of new offences can lead to the offender being returned to custody to serve the remaining sentence.

6.2 Option for Suspended Incarceration

When an offence warrants imprisonment under the custody threshold, a court may issue a suspended sentence instead of immediate detention.

This sentence allows the offender to remain in the community under certain conditions, understanding that failure to adhere to these conditions or committing a new offence during the suspension period will result in imprisonment.

(a) **Suspended Sentence Limits:** The Crown Court has the authority to suspend sentences of up to two years, while the Magistrates' Court can suspend sentences of up to six months.

(b) **Duration of Suspension:** The suspension of the sentence can last for a maximum of two years.

(c) **Additional Conditions:** Courts have the discretion to couple suspended sentences with supplementary requirements resembling those in a community order.

In the event of a breach of the suspended sentence's conditions or the commission of a new offence during its term, the court has several options:

(a) **Activate the entire term** of the imposed initial custodial sentence.

(b) **Activate a portion of the sentence**, accounting for when the offender complied with the suspension.

(c) **Modify the requirements** of the suspended sentence to increase their stringency.

(d) **Extend the duration** of the suspension beyond the original term.

These measures ensure that the suspended sentence serves as both a deterrent and an opportunity for rehabilitation, with clear consequences for non-compliance.

6.3 Imposing Community Orders

Community orders offer courts the option to sentence offenders to penalties served within the community rather than through incarceration. The imposition of a community order is contingent upon the court's judgment that this form of sentence aligns best with the nature of the offence and the offender's circumstances, ensuring the sentence's severity corresponds with the offence's gravity. Often, the court will consider a pre-sentence report from the probation service, which assesses the offender's suitability for a community order and suggests specific conditions.

Community orders can encompass a variety of requirements, such as:

(a) **Unpaid Work:** Mandating the offender to complete a set number of hours of unpaid work in the community.

(b) **Rehabilitative Activities:** Requiring attendance at activities aimed at rehabilitation.

(c) **Educational Programmes:** Enrolment in structured programmes targeting underlying issues related to offending, such as substance abuse or anger management.

(d) **Curfews**: Imposing restrictions on the offender's movements at certain times.

(e) **Exclusion Orders:** Banning the offender from specific locations.

(f) **Residency Requirements:** Obligating the offender to live at a specified address.

(g) **Health-Related Treatments:** Mandating participation in mental health or substance rehabilitation treatments.

Non-compliance with a community order can trigger breach proceedings, which may result in modifying the order to include stricter conditions or, in some cases, replacing the community order with a custodial sentence.

This framework of community orders aims to facilitate the offender's reintegration into society and reduce the likelihood of reoffending while still imposing a punitive element proportionate to the offence.

6.4 Monetary Penalties

Courts have the discretion to levy financial penalties on offenders. A fine can be the sole penalty or part of a broader sentencing package, except when paired with a discharge.

In some instances, the court may determine that no further penalty is warranted beyond the formal recognition of the offence, leading to a discharge. An absolute discharge indicates no additional penalty, while a conditional discharge stipulates that the defendant must avoid further offences for a designated period (up to three years), failing which they risk re-sentencing for the initial offence.

A first-time offender, Jane is convicted of shoplifting items worth $30 from a local store. The court decided that imposing a fine or custodial sentence was unnecessary due to the low value of the stolen items and Jane's previous good character. Instead, the court grants a conditional discharge for 12 months. This means Jane faces no immediate penalty but will be re-sentenced for the shoplifting charge if she commits another offence within the following year.

6.5 Resolving Disputes on Guilt Admission

There may be occasions where a defendant is willing to plead guilty but disputes specific facts of the prosecution's case. In such scenarios, the defendant can propose a plea on a factual basis that they admit to. If the trial concurs that the defendant's account reflects the crime's severity, sentencing can proceed accordingly.

Conversely, if the prosecution challenges the defendant's version, the court will conduct a Newton hearing to resolve the factual discrepancies. This mini-trial involves witness testimonies to ascertain the truth. The outcome of a Newton hearing affects the defendant's entitlement to a reduced sentence for pleading guilty: a result favouring the prosecution negates the plea credit, whereas a result in the defendant's favour preserves it.

Mike pleads guilty to assault but insists he acted in self-defence after being provoked, which the prosecution disputes, claiming Mike was the aggressor. Unable to agree on the facts, the court holds a Newton hearing.

Witnesses who saw the altercation testify, and the judge determines that Mike was provoked, mitigating his culpability. As a result, Mike maintains the credit for his guilty plea and receives a reduced sentence reflecting the circumstances established during the hearing.

CHAPTER 10. APPEAL PROCEDURES

If a defendant believes that the verdict or sentence in their case is unjust, they have the right to seek an appeal. Conversely, prosecutorial rights to challenge a case outcome are significantly more constrained.

1. Challenging Magistrates' Court Decisions in the Crown Court

Right of the Defendant to Appeal:

A defendant convicted guilty at a trial has the prerogative to challenge either the conviction or the sentence in the Crown Court. However, if the defendant entered a guilty plea, they are limited to appealing only against the sentence. The prosecution does not have the privilege of appeal following a Magistrates' Court decision.

Appeal Submission Process:

To initiate an appeal, the defendant must file a written notice with the court that delivered the original verdict or sentence within 21 days. While it's not mandatory to articulate the reasons for the appeal at this stage, as the Crown Court cannot refuse the appeal on this basis, it is customary to outline the grounds for the appeal.

The Crown Court's Review:

A judge from the Crown Court, accompanied by two to four magistrates, oversees the appeal, which entails a full rehearing that may include new evidence. The Crown Court holds the authority to either mitigate or amplify the sentence from the original decision. It should be noted that the Crown Court's sentencing capacity is bound by the limits applicable to the Magistrates' Court. The Crown Court is vested with the authority to levy costs against the appellant should the appeal not succeed.

2. Seeking High Court Review of Magistrates' Court Decisions

The prosecution and the defence are entitled to escalate an appeal from the Magistrates' Court to the Divisional Court (a branch of the High Court) through a process known as "case stated." This type of appeal focuses on legal errors or jurisdictional overreach rather than factual disputes.

(a) **Grounds for Appeal:** The appeal is predicated on asserting that the original court's decision was legally incorrect or exceeded its jurisdictional authority.

(b) **Filing the Appeal:** The appealing party must submit a written application to the Magistrates' Court that delivered the decision within 21 days. This submission must clearly state the legal question that is being challenged.

(c) **Hearing Dynamics:** The Divisional Court, typically comprising three judges, will conduct the appeal. The proceeding revolves around legal argumentation without a retrial of the factual evidence presented in the original case.

The "case stated" process is a form of judicial review that scrutinises the application and interpretation of the law, ensuring the lower court's decision aligns with legal precedents and statutory frameworks.

3. Challenging Crown Court Decisions

Defendants have the right to contest their conviction or sentence from the Crown Court before the Court of Appeal. This process necessitates obtaining permission to appeal, which can be authorised by the trial judge at the Crown Court or by a single judge at the Court of Appeal. To initiate this, a notice must be filed with the convicting court within 28 days post-judgment, which is then reviewed by a judge who determines the viability of the appeal. Should the initial leave to appeal be denied, the defendant can request a reassessment from the full Court of Appeal.

Grounds for Conviction Appeals:

An appeal against a conviction must argue that the verdict is 'unsafe', which can stem from improper evidence handling, judicial bias, or procedural errors during the trial. If the Court of Appeal deems the conviction unsound, they possess several remedial options, including acquittal, ordering a retrial, or altering the sentence to reflect different or lesser charges.

Basis for Sentence Appeals:

An appeal against a sentence can argue that the conviction was legally incorrect, inherently flawed, or excessively harsh. The Court of Appeal may adjust or overturn the sentence but cannot impose a harsher penalty than the original one. Any revised sentence is considered to be effective from the date of the original sentencing.

Opportunities for Prosecution Appeals:

The prosecution's ability to appeal is restricted. While they cannot challenge a jury's acquittal, they can appeal certain judicial decisions made during the trial, such as rulings on the admissibility of evidence. Additionally, if the Attorney General believes a sentence is excessively lenient, they can refer the case to the Court of Appeal.

4. Pathway to the Supreme Court

Appeals can be escalated from the Court of Appeal to the Supreme Court, contingent upon two prerequisites: an appeal permission granted by either the Court of Appeal or the Supreme Court and a certification from the Court of Appeal confirming that the appeal encompasses a point of law of broad public significance.

CHAPTER 11. JUDICIAL PROCESS FOR MINORS

The Youth Court operates under the Magistrates' Court umbrella and specifically handles cases involving individuals from the age of criminal responsibility—10 years old—up to 17 years old.

Here's an **overview of the Youth Court procedures:**

(a) **Closed Proceedings:** Unlike other courts, Youth Court hearings are not open to the public to protect young individuals' privacy.

(b) **Media Access with Restrictions:** While the press may attend, they are under strict limitations to prevent revealing the youth's identity in the proceedings.

(c) **Informality of Proceedings:** The Youth Court is characterised by its informality, aiming to make the legal process less intimidating for young individuals. Legal representatives remain seated when addressing the court, and efforts are made to use easily understandable language.

1. Authority and Continuity

(a) **Age Considerations:** The Youth Court has procedures to deal with situations where a youth turns 18 during their case. Depending on the circumstances, the Youth Court may either see the case to its conclusion or transfer it to the adult Magistrates' Court.

(b) **Sentencing Scope:** Despite the transfer of an individual who reaches the age of majority during proceedings, the range of sentencing options mirrors that of the adult court, ensuring that the severity of the offence is appropriately addressed.

2. Mandatory Referral to Crown Court

Certain serious offences committed by youths necessitate their trial and sentencing at the Crown Court due to the gravity of the crimes.

These include:

(a) **Major Violations:** Offences such as murder, attempted murder, manslaughter, and specific firearm offences.

(b) **Severe Categories of Crime:** Designated violent, sexual, or terrorism-related offences where the youth offender is assessed as posing a significant danger to the public.

3. Handling of Grave Crimes

The term "grave crime" refers to offences that, if committed by an adult, would be eligible for a sentence of 14 years or more.

Examples include robbery, rape, and certain specific offences involving firearms or sexual misconduct.

The following considerations guide the Youth Court's approach to these offences:

(a) **Jurisdiction Assessment:** The Youth Court evaluates whether its sentencing capabilities are sufficient to address the seriousness of the offence. It retains jurisdiction for cases where it deems its sentencing powers adequate.

(b) **Criteria for Crown Court Referral:** Cases are transferred to the Crown Court when the Youth Court determines that its maximum sentencing authority is inadequate for the offence's gravity, suggesting that a longer duration of detention might be necessary.

(c) **Threshold for Declining Jurisdiction:** The Youth Court must believe there is a significant likelihood of imposing a custodial sentence exceeding two years to justify transferring the case to the Crown Court.

This procedural framework ensures that youth offenders accused of serious crimes are tried in a court setting appropriate to the offence's severity while considering the unique aspects of youth justice.

4. Trial Procedures for Youths Charged with Adults

When a youth is jointly charged with an adult, the venue for their trial is determined by the adult co-defendant's trial location:

(a) **Crown Court Trials:** If the adult co-defendant is set to be tried in the Crown Court, the youth will similarly be sent to the Crown Court. This ensures that all parties involved in the same set of offences are tried in the same court, facilitating a unified examination of the case facts and circumstances.

(b) **Magistrates' Court Trials:** If the adult co-defendant's case is being heard in the Magistrates' Court, the youth will also stand trial alongside the adult in the Magistrates' Court. This arrangement allows for consolidating related cases, streamlining the legal process.

This approach aims to maintain consistency in the legal proceedings and ensure that all individuals charged in connection with the same incident are tried in a manner that reflects their collective involvement in the alleged offences.

5. Guidelines for Sentencing Youth Offenders

The sentencing of children and young people is governed by detailed guidelines emphasising rehabilitative over punitive responses.

These guidelines, applicable in both Magistrates' and Crown Courts, outline:

(a) **Available Sentencing Options for Youths:** Various sentencing options tailored to young offenders' developmental needs and rehabilitation prospects exist. These range from non-custodial measures, such as youth rehabilitation orders, to custodial sentences for more serious offences, with a strong preference for sentences that support rehabilitation.

(b) **Sentencing Objectives for Youths:** The overarching goal of sentencing in youth cases is to prevent further offending. This involves a shift in focus from the offence to the offender, recognising the importance of addressing the underlying factors contributing to delinquent behaviour.

The guidelines advocate for the following:

(a) **Rehabilitation**: Encouraging measures that facilitate the young offender's reintegration into society and help them lead a law-abiding life.

(b) **Minimising Criminalisation:** Avoiding unnecessary criminalisation of youths, which can have long-term detrimental effects on their future opportunities and propensity for reoffending.

(c) **Responsibility**: Encouraging young offenders to acknowledge and take responsibility for their actions, fostering a sense of accountability.

This approach reflects a comprehensive understanding of the unique circumstances of young offenders, emphasising the importance of their rehabilitation and the potential for positive development.

5.1 Referral Orders

Referral orders are a specific sentencing option used for young offenders, and they play a critical role in the youth justice system.

Here's an overview of how they operate:

(a) **Mandatory Issuance:** Referral orders are obligatory for young offenders who plead guilty to an offence that can result in imprisonment and who have not been previously convicted (unless the court considers a custodial sentence or an absolute discharge).

(b) **Conditional Issuance:** These orders may be considered in cases where the youth pleads guilty to some charges but not others or if they have received a referral order previously.

(c) **Inapplicability**: Referral orders are not an option if a youth pleads not guilty yet is convicted after a trial.

The essence of a referral order is the youth's engagement with the Youth Offender Panel, including youth offending team members and community volunteers. The panel convenes with the young person and their guardians to devise a tailored contract, lasting between three to twelve

months, to rectify the offending behaviour, address underlying issues, and, where possible, make amends to the victim.

Should the young person re-offend during the term of
the referral order or fail to comply with its terms, the
court is vested with the discretion to let the order continue with modifications or revoke it, opting to pass a different sentence deemed suitable. This mechanism of referral
orders underscores the youth justice system's commitment
to rehabilitation and restorative justice.

5.2 Youth Rehabilitation Orders

Youth Rehabilitation Orders (YROs) are a flexible sentencing option that the Youth Court can impose, with a
duration of up to three years. The order can be tailored
with various requirements to address the specific needs of
the young offender, including:

(a) **Supervision**: Regular meetings with a probation
officer.

(b) **Unpaid Work:** Up to 240 hours for those aged 16
and above.

(c) **Activity Requirements:** Engaging in activities to
make amends or address behavioural issues.

(d) **Programme Requirements:** Participation in structured programs targeting the underlying issues related to the offence, like anger management.

(e) **Curfew and Exclusion:** Restrictions on movements to encourage rehabilitation.

(f) **Residence Requirements:** Stipulations on living arrangements to ensure a stable environment conducive to reform.

5.3 Detention and Training Orders

The Youth Court's custodial sentence is encapsulated in Detention and Training Orders (DTOs) with the following stipulations:

(a) **Ineligibility for the Youngest:** DTOs are unavailable for defendants aged 10 and 11.

(b) **Conditions for 12 to 14-year-olds:** DTOs are reserved for those considered persistent offenders, defined as having been sentenced thrice for imprisonable offences.

(c) **Availability for 15 to 17-year-olds:** Any offender within this age bracket can be sentenced to a

DTO if the seriousness of the case demands a custodial sentence.

The duration of a DTO ranges from four months to two years, with the first half spent in detention and the latter half under supervision. The Youth Offending Team determines the specifics of the supervision. Non-compliance with the terms during the supervision period can result in the youth being ordered to serve the remainder of the sentence in detention.

These sentencing structures reflect a dual approach in youth justice: fostering rehabilitation while holding young offenders accountable for their actions.

CONCLUSION

As we conclude this comprehensive journey through the Criminal Practice Law Guide for the SQE1 exam, reflecting on the extensive knowledge and understanding you have gained is essential.

This guide has taken you through the intricate labyrinth of legal services regulation, professional conduct, and the ethical responsibilities of solicitors, providing you with a solid foundation for your upcoming SQE1 examination and future legal practice.

We wish you the very best in your SQE1 examination and your future endeavours in the legal field. We hope you find success, fulfilment, and the opportunity to contribute significantly to pursuing justice.

REFERENCES

Hutton, S. (2023). Criminal Practice. The University of Law.

Ormerod, D., Perry, D. (2024). Blackstone's Criminal Practice.

ABOUT AUTHORS

Anastasia & Andrew Vialichka have authored a revered collection of study guides and quizzes (metexam.co.uk), addressing the full spectrum of topics tested by the Solicitors Qualifying Examination (SQE). Their portfolio encompasses thorough treatments of *Business Law and Practice, Dispute Resolution, Contract, Tort, Legal System of England and Wales, Constitutional and Administrative Law and EU Law, Legal Services, Property Law and Practice, Wills and the Administration of Estates, Solicitors Accounts, Land Law, Trusts, Criminal Law and Practice,* as well as *Equity.*

The authors' works are not only informational but also innovative, incorporating AI-based technology to enhance test preparation. This modern approach tailors learning to individual styles, aiding students to master both the theory and practice required for the SQE.

www.ingramcontent.com/pod-product-compliance
Lightning Source LLC
Chambersburg PA
CBHW061240220326
41599CB00028B/5493